10Secrets
Wise Parents Know

10 Secrets

Wise Parents Know

Tried and True Things You Can Do to Raise
Faithful, Confident, Responsible Children

Brent L. Top & Bruce A. Chadwick

DESERET
BOOK
SALT LAKE CITY, UTAH

Library of Congress Cataloging-in-Publication Data

Top, Brent L.
    10 secrets wise parents know : tried and true things you can do to raise faithful, confident, responsible children / Brent L. Top, Bruce A. Chadwick.
        p.   cm.
    Includes index.
    ISBN 1-59038-330-3 (pbk.)
    1. Child rearing—Moral and ethical aspects. 2. Child rearing—Religious aspects—Christianity. 3. Child rearing—United States. I. Title: Ten secrets wise parents know. II. Chadwick, Bruce A. III. Title.
    HQ769.T5787 2004
    649'.1—dc22   2004017701

Printed in the United States of America   54459
Malloy Lithographing Incorporated, Ann Arbor, MI

10   9   8   7   6   5   4   3   2   1

To our children and grandchildren

Contents

Introduction

As parents, we all have felt a commingling of emotions when a newborn child is placed in our arms for the first time. We feel joy and excitement. Our highest hopes and aspirations are reflected in the eyes of that beautiful baby. But anxious emotions flood over us as well. The sense of responsibility can be overwhelming, and we ask ourselves, "What do we do now?"

We confront this question not only in those first hours and days with our newborn but also in the years that lie ahead. In every stage of our child's development—whenever we encounter opposition and challenges in our child rearing—we ask the question anew. Unfortunately, the answer isn't always as clear or forthcoming as we would like.

"My parents have no idea how hard it is to be a teenager today," one LDS young man declared. Undoubtedly, his observation is accurate. Yet his parents and perhaps all parents could similarly declare, "My children have no idea how hard it is to be a parent today." Rearing children is a difficult and demanding, yet profoundly rewarding, responsibility. It is a sacred work, but it is *work* nonetheless—hard work.

Have you ever noticed that when we purchase a new vehicle or home appliance, we receive a detailed book of instructions, a maintenance schedule, and often a money-back guarantee? Even articles of clothing come with directions for their proper care, including water temperature for washing and instructions for ironing. Much to our periodic consternation, no such directions exist for rearing children.

There are no fail-safe steps that, if followed, will automatically result in perfect families. There is no warranty that allows us to return disobedient or imperfect children and exchange them for a better model. (This might be appealing to some parents with "turbulent teens" or children in their "terrible twos.") Despite this apparent lack of guarantees, there are guiding principles that provide both help and hope to parents in this trying and tumultuous time for families.

For more than a decade, we have studied Latter-day Saint families and high school youth. We have sought answers to questions that are frequently asked by LDS parents who conscientiously strive to rear righteous children in an increasingly wicked world.

- Is it better to raise children in the heart of "Zion" or in the mission field? Does *where* we live make a difference in how our children turn out?
- What role does religion play in helping our children resist temptation? How can the Church help them meet the spiritual challenges of the day? What can we do to help them better live the principles of the gospel?
- What can we do to counterbalance the negative influence of peers on our children? How can we help our children develop positive friendships?
- How can we have a more loving and harmonious home—a family that exhibits more affection and respect and less contention? What can we do to keep our children close to us and to each other?
- How can we balance the need to discipline our children with the need to be loving and supportive? What rules should we have for our family? Is it possible to be too strict?
- What can we do to help our children become

mature, responsible, competent, and emotionally healthy young adults?

One of the primary motivations for our research has been the mixed signals that parents receive from the many voices of the not-so-family-friendly culture of modern society. Traditional family values that have long been the basic building blocks of successful homes are now challenged and even ridiculed.

For example, one recent book titled *The Nurture Assumption,* by Judith Rich Harris, received considerable media attention and was hailed in some circles as the best news stressed-out parents had heard in years. The author advocates guilt-free parenting because, according to her theory, parents have no influence on their children aside from the genetic code they transmit at conception. Parenting thus becomes a one-time biological act, not a lifetime mission of nurturing. The author contends that peers, not parents, will determine what our children do and how they turn out. As a result, the author declares that fathers and mothers can quit trying so hard to be good parents because good parenting doesn't matter any more than does bad parenting— with the obvious exception of the terrible damage incurred by physical or sexual abuse.

Teaching values to and spending significant time with our children, according to this theory, doesn't yield any significant results. High-intensity, hands-on parenting simply isn't cost-effective. We can almost hear the father of lies, the author of such destructive philosophies, saying, "Don't worry about your sacred obligations as a parent. It doesn't matter what you do anyway. Use your time to do what you want to do. You deserve it! Go golfing!"

Some social scientists have postulated through the years that, while parents *may* matter in child development, religion has *no* significant impact on the strength of a family or on the behavior of a child. Others dismiss faith and religious values as irrelevant in today's society. Still others acknowledge that religion does affect behavior but that its impact is sociological, not spiritual. And some are hostile toward religion, claiming that it is actually detrimental to emotional development and mental health. They contend that religious beliefs and values have power only within a social context—a culture of religious involvement. They argue that religion is something that happens *around* you, not *within* you.

These conclusions just didn't sit right with us. We know from personal experience and observation that parents do, indeed, matter—more than mere biological conception—in the process of rearing righteous and responsible children. Moreover, we know that religion has a far more expansive influence on individuals, homes, and families than many in the world would have us believe. We know that this power of faith is internal, not just external; that it is spiritual, not just cultural. Yet we wanted empirical evidence to substantiate or refute these assumptions. As a result, we conducted a ten-year study that spanned several geographical areas, three nations, two languages, diverse cultural and racial backgrounds, and a wide variety of challenges facing both parents and youth today.

We surveyed more than five thousand Latter-day Saint teens from the United States, Great Britain, and Mexico. From this research we gleaned valuable information concerning the religious beliefs and practices of LDS youth, the kinds of temptations and peer pressures they face, and what their parents are doing in the home to help them. Several publications, directed to academics as well as to a general Church audience, have reported the findings of this study,[1] which revealed the following important conclusions:

- It doesn't matter so much *where* we raise our children as it does *what* we do in our home.
- Even though peer influences have enormous power, they are not the only (or even the most important) influences in the lives of our children. Faith and family can also have significant power in the lives of young people—sufficient to minimize or override the impact of peer pressure.
- Children who have internalized gospel principles and developed their own personal

spirituality are better equipped to resist temptation, are less likely to engage in delinquent and immoral behavior, have a better sense of self-worth, and do better in school.

• Children who come from homes where parents seek to maintain a close personal relationship with them through love and support are more responsive to parental teachings and discipline.

Obviously, none of these findings was previously unknown. We haven't done anything earth-shaking like discover fire, explore a new continent, or invent the wheel. What we have observed from our research concerning the establishment of strong families is nothing more than what the gospel and the prophets and apostles have long taught. We did not initiate our research with some grand design to scientifically *prove* the teachings of the Church concerning families. They don't need that kind of validation. But our scientific results do demonstrate two things.

First, they clearly refute the notion that neither parents nor religion can exert much meaningful influence in the lives of adolescents. It is clear that faith and family—gospel internalization, personal spirituality, and testimony, coupled with a strong relationship with parents—have a powerful protective influence in the lives of our children in this spiritually and physically dangerous world. Second, we can conclude from our research—even though academics wouldn't accept this as the final word—that following the counsel of Church leaders and seeking to better live gospel principles really does work. Families are strengthened, unbreakable bonds of love and support are fortified, and children and parents alike, clothed in the armor of God, are able to "withstand the evil day" (D&C 27:15). The gospel provides parents and grandparents with an ample supply of both *help* and *hope.*

The statistical results of our study were *interesting*—at least to social scientists and statisticians who love such things as beta coefficients, multivariate correlations, and structural-equation models. But some things were clearly *important:* practical suggestions and insights that can help mothers and fathers in their significant and sacred responsibilities at home. Several important parenting practices and principles repeatedly surfaced both from the statistics and from the hundreds upon hundreds of comments we received from the teens surveyed.

To help us further understand what we learned from these five thousand LDS teens, we also surveyed one thousand LDS young adults ages nineteen to twenty-eight. With a few years of experience and some twenty-twenty hindsight under their belts, these young adults were able to identify the things their parents did that helped them resist temptation and successfully meet the spiritual challenges they faced. These young adults also identified things their parents did that were counterproductive to raising righteous children, and they noted things they wished their parents had done in their homes.

In addition, we surveyed several hundred "experienced parents," ranging in age from early thirties to late eighties. Included in this group were grandparents who had already raised their families and young parents who were raising toddlers and teens. Each parent provided important insights into successful parenting practices. These experienced parents identified those things they did (or are doing) that were most successful in establishing strong family relationships and rearing righteous children. They also identified things they wished they had done differently in rearing their families. Both groups—the young adults who were not yet parents and the experienced parents—were also asked to list what they considered to be the five most important traits of successful parents.

From this mountain of information and insight, including the inspired counsel from modern prophets and apostles, we have identified ten principles that can strengthen any family. The purpose of this book is to highlight those ten principles in a practical, down-to-earth, yet inspiring way that will be both helpful and hopeful. While it is true that there are no money-back guarantees when it comes to parenting, these principles are pretty close to being fail-safe. We know this to be true—not just because of our years of research but also because we have seen these principles in action (or inaction, as the case may be) in our own homes and with our own children and grandchildren.

As we have worked on this project, thought about these principles, and shared them in scores of meetings, conferences, workshops, and firesides, we have often said, "We wish we had known that twenty years ago," or "We should have done that better when the kids were young." It is not our intent to send anyone on a parental guilt trip. We all have and probably will continue to have our share of regrets. Every parent makes mistakes, and every family is dysfunctional in some way because we are all mortal. Regret alone, however, doesn't necessarily bring change or strengthen families. Resolve coupled with action—trying to be a better parent—does. How grateful we are that we have learned one of the most important lessons for parents: It's never too late! It's never too late to try to be a good parent. It's never too late to express love in word and deed to our families. Gospel teachings and covenants testify that we are never really *done* being parents—here or hereafter.

We could also say that it is never too *early* to be a good parent. Virtually all of our research dealt with adolescent youth. We looked at those things that can help parents and youth leaders deal with their teens and the difficult challenges they face. In the process, one thing kept coming back to us again and again. It was the thought that if we wait to incorporate these principles and suggestions until our children are teenagers, our parental efforts will be severely handicapped. Like shaping or straightening a tree, it is easier to apply these principles when our children are young. Doing so will lessen the need for drastic measures when they hit their turbulent teens.

As the wise author of the book of Proverbs declared, "Train up a child in the way he should go: and when he is old, he will not depart from it" (Proverbs 22:6).

Note

1.   See Brent L. Top and Bruce A. Chadwick, *Rearing Righteous Youth of Zion* (Salt Lake City: Bookcraft, 1998); "Protecting Purity," *BYU Magazine,* Summer 2003, 46–54; "Spirituality and Self-Worth: The Role of Religion in Shaping Teens' Self-Image," *The Religious Educator* 4, no. 2 (2003): 77–93; "'Seek Learning Even by Study and Also by Faith': The Relationship Between Personal Religiosity and Academic Achievement among Latter-day Saint High School Students," *The Religious Educator* 2, no. 2 (2001): 121–37; "Helping Teens Stay Strong," *Ensign,* March 1999, 26–34; "Raising Righteous Children in a Wicked World," *BYU Magazine,* Summer 1998, 41–51; "Family, Religion, and Delinquency among LDS Youth," in *Religion, Mental Health, and the Latter-day Saints,* ed. Daniel K. Judd (Provo, Utah: Religious Studies Center, Brigham Young University, 1999), 129–68; "The Power of the Word: Religion, Family, Friends,

and Delinquent Behavior of LDS Youth," *BYU Studies* 33, no. 2 (1993): 293–310; "Religiosity and Delinquency among LDS Adolescents," *Journal for the Scientific Study of Religion* 32, no. 1 (March 1993): 51–67.

Chapter 1

Build a Household of Faith

Every gardener knows that a fertile, well-prepared seedbed is vital for healthy plants. If the soil isn't properly prepared, the seeds will not sprout—no matter how good they are. Once the seedlings break the surface of the soil, there is much more to do. The gardener must nurture and nourish the young plants, seeing that they receive adequate water and sunshine. The gardener also must be vigilant in protecting the seedlings from invasions of nutrient-robbing weeds or destructive pests. This is not only a physical principle but also a spiritual one that has important applications to families.

The Book of Mormon prophet Alma taught that the seed of faith must have a fertile seedbed in the heart and soul. After we have "given place" to the seed so that our faith has sprouted and begun to grow, the seed must be patiently and consistently nurtured and protected (Alma 32). It works the same way in the lives of our children. The gospel of Jesus Christ is the good seed that we desire to be planted in the hearts of our children. We, as parents, are the gardeners, and our home, President Gordon B. Hinckley has declared, "is the seedbed of all true virtue. If proper values are not learned in the home, they are not likely to be learned anywhere."[1]

The seed of faith, as the Book of Mormon testifies, can grow into a strong tree of spiritual strength and personal testimony. For that to happen, however, the seedling must be carefully nourished. The Lord has given parents the primary responsibility for the spiritual nourishment of their children.

> And again, inasmuch as parents have children in Zion, or in any of her stakes which are organized, that teach them not to understand the doctrine of repentance, faith in Christ the Son of the living God, and of baptism and the gift of the Holy Ghost by the laying on of the hands, when eight years old, the sin be upon the heads of the parents.
>
> For this shall be a law unto the inhabitants of Zion, or in any of her stakes which are organized. And their children shall be baptized for the remission of their sins when eight years old, and receive the laying on of the hands. And they shall teach their children to pray, and to walk uprightly before the Lord. (D&C 68:25–28)

King Benjamin taught his people anciently—and his teachings have just as much meaning and application to us today—that parents have the obligation to provide their children with both temporal necessities and spiritual necessities.

> And ye will not suffer your children that they go hungry, or naked; neither will ye suffer that they transgress the laws of God, and fight and quarrel one with another, and serve the devil, who is the master of sin, or who is the evil spirit which hath been spoken of by our fathers, he being an enemy to all righteousness.
>
> But ye will teach them to walk in the ways of truth and soberness; ye will teach them to love one another, and to serve one another. (Mosiah 4:14–15)

The Lord has given this sacred and solemn responsibility to parents not simply as a commandment or a test of obedience. As with all of God's laws, there are promised blessings attached—blessings that can be realized here and now, as well as in the eternities.

An interesting example of this concept can be found in the commandment given to the early Saints to build a temple in Kirtland, Ohio. Interestingly, the Lord didn't come right out and say, "Build a temple." Rather, he asked them to "establish a house, even a house of prayer, a house of fasting, a house of faith, a house of learning, a house of glory, a house of order, a house of God" (D&C 88:119). The blessings promised the Saints for obedience to this commandment included an outpouring of God's spirit, great spiritual learning, great power, and spiritual manifestations (D&C 109:12–23, 34–39).

Just as the Lord promised the institutional Church great blessings if it would establish "a house of God," so too will he pour out blessings upon individual homes and families if they, likewise, establish "a house of God." As temples enable God's children to be endowed with power, so our own homes—houses of faith—can endow our children with a spiritual power and influence that protects them in these trying times. The Apostle Paul spoke of this protective endowment as the "armour of God" that enables us "to stand against the wiles of the devil" (Ephesians 6:11).

Wouldn't it be nice if we could buy from the Church distribution center "Armour of God" spray cans or "Shield of Faith" soap that we could use on our children to protect them against temptation? Unfortunately, or fortunately, it doesn't work that way. The armor of God and the shield of faith cannot be applied merely from the *outside*. They must be developed from the *inside*. Their development is not a one-time event but rather an ongoing process that requires determination, hard work, and patience.

Creating a spiritual environment in the home provides the best opportunity for our children to develop a shield of faith within themselves. In our study of effective parenting, experienced parents who had already raised their children as well as young adults who could look back on their upbringing identified the spiritual environment of their homes as the single most important factor in raising righteous children.

Repeatedly, we found significant statistical evidence showing that what mothers and fathers do in their homes to help cultivate the religious development of their children has great power to influence righteous behavior and minimize the effects of negative peer pressure. The power of faith within the family unit is indisputable. What, then, can we do to foster faith and strengthen spirituality within our children so that they will "be able to quench all the fiery darts of the wicked" (D&C 27:17)?

Make Religion a Way of Life

Through the years, sociological studies have examined the effects of religion on families and on the behavior of adolescents. The results have been mixed, at best. A common conclusion has been that religiosity has little, if any, effect. It is interesting to note, however, that most of the studies defined religiosity merely in terms of affiliation with a church and attendance at Sunday meetings. If that is all there is to religiosity, it is not surprising that religion would seem to have no significant effect.

In later studies, however, religiosity has been

found to affect behavior and deter delinquency. These studies defined religiosity more broadly to include such things as personal spirituality, religious conviction, and private religious behaviors. A growing body of evidence shows that when religion is more than mere church attendance, it offers protective power.

The word *religion* shares the same linguistic root as the word *ligament—ligare,* which means to "connect" or "hold together." Religion exerts power in our families when it is fully attached to or connected with every aspect of our lives. Only when we as parents take the gospel seriously in all aspects of our lives will our children take it seriously and internalize its principles in their lives.

"The home and family have vital roles in cultivating personal faith and testimony," Elder M. Russell Ballard declared. "The family is the basic unit of society; the best place for individuals to build faith and strong testimonies is in *righteous homes filled with love.* . . . Strong, faithful families have the best opportunity to produce strong, faithful members of the Church."[2]

Many young people have identified the spiritual environment of their homes and the deep religious convictions of their parents as the primary means whereby they gained their own spiritual strength. "My parents put the Lord first in their lives," one teenager observed. "The most important thing that has helped me internalize gospel principles in my life has been seeing how the gospel and Church are central in their lives." Another stated, "My parents taught me the importance of the gospel by how they lived their lives. The gospel is everything to them."

One of the most significant things we can do to demonstrate the importance of religion in daily life and to establish a spiritual environment in our home is to hold family prayer. Not only do our children see our love for and devotion to God through this practice, but they also hear expressions of gratitude for the Lord's blessings and petitions in their behalf. Through family prayer, our children learn important and lasting gospel lessons. Elder John H. Groberg declared:

> I know of no single activity that has more potential for unifying our families and bringing more love and divine direction into our homes than consistent, fervent family prayer.
>
> Think of the power for good as you gather your family together and thank God for all of his blessings. Think of the eternal significance of daily thanking him for each member of your family and asking him to guide and bless and protect each one. Think of the strength that will come to your family as, daily, one member or another pours out his or her soul in love to God for other family members . . .
>
> We all want more love and unity in our families. We all need more help with some who

may be wayward or in special need. We all desire more assurance of divine guidance and direction.

I promise you that as you consistently and fervently pray as a family, and as each member takes his or her turn and sincerely prays for others, impressions will come as to what you individually should do to help others. Thus, you can, in family prayer, receive personal and family revelation as to how to love and serve one another.[3]

When religion permeates every aspect of our lives—holding them together like a ligament—we go to church, have family prayer and scripture study, and serve our fellowmen, not because it is what we have to do but rather because it is what we are all about. It is our life, not just an activity. The gospel is our daily walk and talk, not just something we learn about in Sunday School. The foundation for a "house of faith" is laid with such things as regular attendance at Church together as a family, daily family prayer and scripture study, faithful service in Church callings and assignments, temple attendance, and service to our fellowmen. In a "house of faith" the importance of the gospel is manifest by sharing spiritual feelings, talking about gospel messages, and expressing gratitude to God—and not just on Sunday. One young woman remembered:

> As my dad washed the dishes in the sink or worked outside in the yard, sometimes out of the blue he would say, "Heavenly Father, thank you for this beautiful day," or "Thank you, Father, for

my daughter Amy." This impressed me, and it taught me that I could approach the Lord and have spiritual feelings at any time and in any setting.

The spiritual environment of the home can also be strengthened by displaying gospel-related pictures, such as the temple or the Savior. Our children must know, however, that these pictures represent something spiritually significant in our lives and are not just home furnishings. Likewise, the standard works, Church magazines, and Church videos and DVDs can help make our home "a house of God," but only if we use them consistently.

In a way, our children learn by osmosis—absorbing like sponges from the spiritual environment in which they live, the examples they observe, and the things they daily experience. This is why real religion cannot be neatly compartmentalized into a single day of the week or into some ritualistic act. Spiritual osmosis may occur with our children as we create an environment conducive to religion and make the gospel the cornerstone of our family. But we cannot sit passively by and hope that they absorb religion.

"Don't just assume your children will somehow get the drift of your beliefs on their own," said Elder Jeffrey R. Holland.[4] Establishing "a house of faith" requires instruction as well as environment. As the scriptures declare, parents have an obligation to be anxiously engaged in teaching the "doctrine of the kingdom" to their children (D&C 88:77).

Teach the Gospel

"How would you pass the test, parents, if your family was isolated from the Church and *you* had to supply all religious training?" Elder A. Theodore Tuttle asked. "Have you become so dependent on others that you do little or nothing at home? Tell me, how much of the *gospel* would your children know if all they knew were what they had been taught at home? Ponder that. I repeat, how much of the gospel would *your* children know if all they knew is what they had been taught at home?"[5]

What a sobering thought! How grateful we should be that we are not left totally alone in teaching and training our children. We must not, however, pass the buck to others and abdicate our role as the primary providers of religious instruction and spiritual training for our children.

In a letter addressed to "Members of the Church throughout the World," dated February 11, 1999, the First Presidency declared: "We call upon parents to devote their best efforts to the teaching and rearing of their children in gospel principles which will keep them close to the Church." They further declared that "the home is the basis of a righteous life" and that no other agency, program, or organization can adequately replace parents in fulfilling their "God-given responsibility" of teaching the gospel.[6]

During our many years of studying LDS youth and their families, we have repeatedly witnessed how effective gospel instruction in the home helps to spiritually insulate youth from the many temptations of the world. Young people receive a very real infusion of protective power—more important than just increased doctrinal knowledge—that results from inspired gospel instruction at home.

Recently we asked several hundred young adults, "What did your parents do in raising you that you now appreciate and view as being most significant in helping you become the kind of person you should be?" Scores of comments focused on gospel instruction received at home. Similarly, experienced parents who have already raised their children cited gospel teaching at home as being among the most significant things they did to successfully rear their children. Their experiences—and the experiences of many thousands of parents and youth like them—confirm the inspired counsel of prophets and apostles. Elder Boyd K. Packer said:

> If you want your children to grow spiritually, teach them the doctrines of the gospel. If you want your son to play the piano, it is good to expose him to music. This may give him a feel for it and help greatly in his learning. But this is not enough. There is the practice and the

memorization and the practice and the practice and the practice before he can play it well.

If you want your daughter to learn a language, expose her to those who speak it. She may get a feel for the language, even pick up many words. But this is not enough. She must memorize grammar and vocabulary. She must practice pronunciation. There is rote learning without which she will never speak or write the language fluently.

So it is with the gospel. One may have a feel for it. But some time one must *learn* the doctrine. Here, too, rote learning, practice, memorization, reading, listening, discussion, all become essential. There is no royal road to learning.[7]

A temple becomes "a house of faith" by also being "a house of learning." Likewise, the spiritual development of our children occurs somewhat in proportion to the degree that our homes are spiritual schools with a gospel curriculum founded upon "none other things than that which the prophets and apostles have written, and that which is taught them by the Comforter through the prayer of faith" (D&C 52:9).

It would be easy for us to feel overwhelmed by this sacred obligation. Some of us may feel that we lack sufficient gospel knowledge to properly teach our children. Some of us may feel that we lack teaching skills. Some of us may have additional concerns. All of us have inadequacies, but the Lord has given us the responsibility to teach the gospel to our children nonetheless. Fortunately, the Lord never gives responsibilities without also providing "a way for them that they may accomplish the thing which he commandeth them" (1 Nephi 3:7). The Church has provided us with people, programs, and inspired counsel that can assist us in our responsibilities and make them far less intimidating.

"We counsel parents and children," the First Presidency stated, "to give highest priority to family prayer, family home evening, gospel instruction, and wholesome family activities."[8] Each of these activities helps us to more effectively teach the gospel to our children, but they cannot help us if we don't take advantage of them.

Family Home Evening

"The weekly [family] home evening," Elder Harold B. Lee taught, is "the Lord's way to build the foundation to safeguard our youth against the ills that beset the world."[9] For nearly a century, leaders of the Church have encouraged parents to devote Monday nights "to prayer, singing hymns, songs, instrumental music, scripture reading, family topics, and *specific instruction on the principles of the Gospel*, and on the ethical problems of life."[10]

Not only do all members of the Church know about family home evening, but many other people throughout the world also know about and admire this program for families. With so much having been said and written about the importance of family home evening, you would think that by now every LDS family would be holding it each week.

Our research has shown a direct link between regular family home evening and lower levels of delinquency, drug and alcohol abuse, and premarital sex, as well as increased self-worth and academic improvement. The results are remarkable and indisputable. Doing what the prophets have asked us to do really works! It shouldn't take scientific evidence to convince us of that. The promised blessings are real. Yet our studies have shown that, despite the great benefits that result from family religious practices, less than half (approximately 40 percent) of active LDS families hold regular family home evening. Only about half have regular family prayer, and only about 30 percent hold some form of regular scripture study.

Have you ever noticed that the more spiritually significant our work is, the more the adversary seeks to prevent us from doing it? Consider, for example, how many things seem to go wrong or come up at the last minute when we're preparing to go to the temple. Consider the temptations that arise just before we are supposed to do something important, such as give a priesthood blessing or render some other important service. Satan seems to know, much better than we, that our spiritually significant work will shake the foundation of his kingdom because such work draws us closer to God and makes us more resistant to temptation. No wonder he seeks, in any way he can, to prevent us from holding regular family home evening.

Every family has experienced both fulfillment and frustration associated with family home evening. Sometimes Monday nights can seem more like civil war than "love at home." Brother pinches sister. Sister punches brother and screams, "Stop it!" Pinching, punching, and screaming escalate. Dad yells at the children. Mom begins crying. The Spirit leaves. Someone once observed that family home evening is "a fight that opens with prayer." (Church basketball also fits this description.)

Effective family home evenings do not just automatically happen. They take planning and preparation, but most of all they take perseverance. It is tempting to throw up our hands in disgust at the first signs of contention, resistance, or boredom. We have all asked ourselves, "Why are we doing this when we can't even get along with each other? Why bother to teach when the children don't seem to be listening to a word?"

Success comes from not giving up. Consistently holding family home evening—even when it seems that the kids aren't listening or learning or having any great spiritual experiences—is a spiritual success in itself. More is happening in our children's heads and hearts than we may see at the moment.

The comments of many young people in our study confirm that fact, including the following:

> I know I was a pain in the neck to my parents when it came to family prayer and family home evening. But I am thankful now that they didn't give up. It had more influence upon me than I was willing to admit at the time.
>
> I pretended not to be listening when we had lessons during family night or when we had scripture study, but more sank in than my parents thought.

A mother who had successfully raised her children and is now a grandmother credited family home evening with much of the success she and her husband experienced with their children. "Our lessons weren't always great, but we were consistent in holding home evening," she said. "That is where our children got their gospel foundation. I think it was the most important thing we did in our home."

Others, both young adults and experienced parents, expressed deep regret that family home evening wasn't a more important part of their home life:

> I wish that we had had regular family home evening and family prayer. We did it once in a while, but I wish we would have been more consistent. I probably would have hated it at the time, but now I see its importance.

I wish my parents had taught gospel principles more in our home. To see my parents reading from the scriptures and teaching us from them would have been really helpful as I was growing up.

We should have taken family home evening more seriously. We figured that if we were together at home on Monday nights, that was enough. Now I wish we had taught lessons and talked more openly about spiritual things. I wish my children had heard me talk more at home about my love for the Lord and the gospel and heard me bear my testimony in a family setting.

The gospel was lived in our home, but we didn't have family home evenings. I have since learned that teaching your children the gospel can never be put off until a later time. Establishing the habits of family prayer, home evening, and scripture study when your family is young makes it easier. We found that the opportunities to teach the gospel to our children began to lessen as our children got older and busier.

Family home evening provides parents with a regular opportunity to teach their children from the scriptures and to discuss and apply gospel principles. It is not enough just to keep Monday nights free from outside activities. Neither is it adequate just to be together in the same room or the same house watching *Monday Night Football*. Every family needs fun, social activities, service, and refreshments, but the primary purpose of family home evening is to teach the gospel, bear testimony, express love for the Lord and for each other, and strengthen spirituality. It is the foundation of a house of faith. President Spencer W. Kimball taught:

> Merely going to a show or a party together, or fishing, only half satisfies the real need, but to stay home and teach the children the gospel, the scriptures, and love for each other and love for their parents is most important. . . .
>
> The gospel [is] a family affair. By committing ourselves to having the regular and inspirational family home evening and by carefully planning the content of that evening, we are sending a signal to our children which they will remember forevermore. When thus we give our children of our own time, we are giving of our presence, a gift that is always noticed.
>
> The Home Evening Manual is replete with good suggestions, but it should never replace inspired parental development with regard to what should be done in a particular evening to meet particular needs. If we will feed our families from the gospel garden at home, then what they get at Church meetings can be a rich supplement, but not their only diet.[11]

Family Scripture Study

The spiritual environment of our home is also strengthened through regular scripture study. Through consistent study of the standard works, our families can experience the power of the word. Family scripture study further strengthens our "armour of God" against the "fiery darts" of these spiritually perilous times (Ephesians 6:13, 16).

"Scripture study as individuals and as a family is most fundamental to learning the gospel," President Kimball said. "Daily reading the scriptures *and discussing them together* has long been suggested as a powerful tool against ignorance and the temptations of Satan. This practice will produce great happiness and will help family members love the Lord and his goodness."[12]

It is important to note the phrase "and discussing them together." Sometimes we view family scripture study as some kind of race or something we just have to get through. Without a doubt there is value in reading *through* the scriptures, but there is greater power in teaching *from* the scriptures. Getting through a particular volume of scripture is important, but scripture *comprehension* is more important than *coverage*.

So what if it takes two years or even ten years to read the Book of Mormon as a family? What's important is that we increase our understanding of the gospel and learn what the scriptures *mean*, not just what they *say*. In an educational setting, the lowest level of learning takes place when a student merely reads the textbook with no guidance from a teacher, no discussions, no homework, and no application.

The learning level increases proportionately with guidance from a teacher, class discussions, home-work, and personal application through hands-on experience with the subject matter. Gospel learning and scripture study work much the same way.

In addition to the learning that can take place from this kind of family scripture study, protective power and blessings come to those families that "try the virtue of the word of God" (Alma 31:5). President Marion G. Romney promised:

> I feel certain that if, in our homes, parents will read from the Book of Mormon prayerfully and regularly, both by themselves and with their children, the spirit of that great book will come to permeate our homes and all who dwell therein. The spirit of reverence will increase; mutual respect and consideration for each other will grow. The spirit of contention will depart. Parents will counsel their children in greater love and wisdom. Children will be more responsive and submissive to the counsel of their parents. Righteousness will increase. Faith, hope, and charity—the pure love of Christ—will abound in our homes and lives, bringing in their wake peace, joy, and happiness.[13]

What conscientious parent would not want these promises? The returns from a spiritual home environment fortified by regular family scripture study are so immense that we would be unwise stewards of our children not to invest time, obedience to prophetic counsel, and faith in such dividends.

Informal Gospel Discussions

Not all opportunities to teach the gospel to our children occur on Sundays, Monday evenings, or during early morning scripture study. In fact, some of the most important teaching moments may come at unscheduled times. They may come when a daughter faces a difficult challenge at school or when a son is debating the merits of a mission— anytime a child is wondering or worrying or questioning.

Seizing these teaching moments whenever they occur and talking about the gospel when needed shows our children that the gospel has everyday relevance and application in our lives. Often these informal discussions help our children to better connect the dots, so to speak, and see how the principles of the gospel really fit together and apply to daily life.

We often leave our children with the impression that the only reason we keep the commandments is so we can be worthy of exaltation in the next life. This deferred-gratification approach doesn't help our children understand that the reason we live the gospel is that it blesses our lives here and now, not just hereafter. Perhaps one of the most important functions of gospel discussions, whether formal or informal, is to help our children see that the gospel has relevance, application, and answers for everyday questions, challenges, and problems.

One father, for example, shared with his children at the dinner table some of the challenges of his day. Each evening he would ask, "How would you deal with this?" The children thought they were helping Dad with his work, but in reality Dad was stimulating gospel discussions and helping them see how the gospel can solve real-world problems. One young woman made the following astute observation as to how informal gospel discussions can yield unexpected and unintentional, yet powerful, gospel learning experiences:

> There are two places that I hold dear to my heart and see as great gospel learning places. This may sound strange, but they are my parents' king-size bed and the kitchen table. We almost always ate dinner together, and there we would talk about our daily activities, but there was much more than that. We often would get into in-depth gospel discussions or talk about how we felt about something. Just these little things taught me so much. As for the bed—it had to be a king-size so all six of us kids could fit on it. This was a place where we could talk with Mom and Dad. I received so much comfort, guidance, and spiritual teaching there.

Practice What You Preach

The old adage "I cannot hear what you are saying because your actions speak louder than your words" is certainly true within the walls of a home.

Nothing will undermine our efforts to create a spiritual home environment more than not practicing what we preach. Daily family prayer and scripture study and weekly home evening lessons will seem hollow or trivial to our children if we don't translate what we learn into a comprehensive way of life. To use the language of our kids: "We must walk the walk, not just talk the talk."

This doesn't mean we have to be perfect parents. We're not, and our children know it. They're smart enough to realize that we have weaknesses, and at times we may not be as good as we desire. Parents do serious damage, however, when they go against the very teachings and standards they expect of their children. It seems that our children have a special radar system in their spirits that can detect not only parental hypocrisy but also insincerity.

Many teens who don't notice the clutter and chaos in their bedrooms or the lateness of the hour when they're having fun are quick to observe parental hypocrisy or attempts to live a double standard. When it comes to having "a house of faith" and "a house of God," there can be no double standards! One father remembered how his young son taught him this valuable lesson:

> We had spent most of the snowy Saturday watching videos with our family. Each of the children had picked out their favorite show. We popped popcorn, ate treats, and generally had a

great time. When it came time for bed, we told the kids the party was over and they needed to get ready for sleep.

"But there's one more video to watch," my son announced. "That one is for Mom and me to watch after you guys go to bed," I retorted. "Can't we watch it too?" the other children chimed in. "No, it isn't good for children."

I tried to explain. It was not a bad video or pornographic in any way but of a more mature theme that we didn't want the children to see. I thought I explained it in a reasonable manner. At least until my son asked the question to which I had no good answer. "If it is not good for us, why is it good for you?"

At that moment I realized that it was no longer an issue about movies. It was all about example. His question continues to remind me that what is good for them must be good for me, and what is bad for them is bad for me too. I don't want my children to think that Dad lives a double standard.

If we want our children to have testimonies of the gospel, to internalize its principles, and to live by high standards of purity and integrity, we must do the same. If we want them to be worthy to marry in the temple, we should strive to be temple worthy and demonstrate our love for the temple by frequent attendance. If we want them to study the scriptures and sincerely pray to our Heavenly Father each day, we need to do the same. If we want them to be committed to the gospel and actively involved in the Church, we need to show them the way by our lives—by our activity in the Church and our faith-fulness to callings and covenants. To do otherwise sends the signal to our children that the gospel we teach really isn't all that important to us after all. As a result, they won't take it seriously either.

The spiritual environment of our home and the religious development of our children must begin with us. We can't give what we don't have! Our examples, as parents, are powerful teaching tools, whether we view ourselves as teachers or not. We teach our children—for good or bad—every moment of our lives through every word we speak and every attitude we exhibit and every act we commit. For this reason, we need to "live the gospel as conspicu-ously as [we] can," Elder Jeffrey R. Holland coun-seled. He suggested that we need to periodically ask ourselves what our children know from us:

> Do our children know that we love the scrip-tures? Do they see us reading them and marking them and clinging to them in daily life? Have our children ever unexpectedly opened a closed door and found us on our knees in prayer? Have they heard us not only pray *with* them but also pray *for* them out of nothing more than sheer parental love? Do our children know we believe in fasting as something more than an obligatory first-Sunday-of-the-month hardship? Do they know that we have fasted for them and for their future

on days about which they knew nothing? Do they know we love being in the temple, not least because it provides a bond to them that neither death nor the legions of hell can break? Do they know we love and sustain local and general leaders, imperfect as they are, for their willingness to accept callings they did not seek in order to preserve a standard of righteousness they did not create? Do those children know that we love God with all our heart and that we long to see the face—and fall at the feet—of His Only Begotten Son? I pray they know this.

Brothers and sisters, our children take their flight into the future with our thrust and with our aim. And even as we anxiously watch that arrow in flight and know all the evils that can deflect its course after it has left our hand, nevertheless we take courage in remembering that the most important mortal factor in determining that arrow's destination will be the stability, strength, and unwavering certainty of the holder of the bow.[14]

"Examine yourselves," the Apostle Paul admonished, "whether ye be in the faith" (2 Corinthians 13:5). The questions posed by a modern apostle and the charge to personal introspection by an ancient apostle are relevant to each of us as we seek to establish "a house of faith," "a house of God"—a place where our children will not only be taught gospel principles but will also be spiritually molded into true disciples of the Master.

Someone once wisely observed, "Children seldom *hear* their parents, but they always *emulate* them." The righteous example of parents who have made the gospel the very core of their souls provides their children with a living, breathing object lesson of what true religion, true spirituality, and true gospel living are all about. Many of the young people we have studied through the years have identified the personal example of their parents as the most important influence in their lives:

> My parents' examples of living the teachings of Christ helped me to internalize gospel principles in my own life. Although this may not be very specific, the most important thing was just seeing in them that the gospel and Church were central to their lives. It was evident in every aspect of their lives.

> My parents always set the example of going to Church and holding family prayer and home evening. But more than that, I was impressed by their examples on a personal level. They never swore or saw R-rated movies, they served others, and, most important, they were totally honest regardless of the situation. They really lived the gospel.

During his mortal ministry, Jesus admonished his followers to count the cost of discipleship. He illustrated this principle with the parable of the tower builder:

> For which of you, intending to build a tower,
> sitteth not down first, and counteth the cost,
> whether he have sufficient to finish it? Lest haply,
> after he hath laid the foundation, and is not able
> to finish it, all that behold it begin to mock him,
> Saying, This man began to build, and was not
> able to finish. (Luke 14:28–30)

This certainly applies to building a house of faith—establishing a family on a spiritual foundation of the gospel of Jesus Christ. A house of faith does not automatically just happen and miraculously appear anymore than the tower in the parable. It has to be built, and building always requires a cost for supplies and labor. We count the cost by determining what will be required to establish the kind of spiritual home we desire and then going to work to build it.

The materials from which a house of faith is built—family home evening, prayer, scripture study, Church activities and programs, inspired counsel from living prophets, and myriad other spiritual helps for families—have been freely provided by the Lord, but they don't assemble themselves. We must provide the labor by consistently teaching the gospel in our homes by precept and example. It is a labor-intensive process that requires us to keep at it—not stopping or giving in or giving up when the construction seems a little slow or when we encounter unexpected difficulties.

Establishing "a house of faith" is not an easy

task, but it is worth the effort. The blessings far out-weigh the challenges. The protection and promises exceed the problems. President Howard W. Hunter testified:

> Without doubt there are significant challenges facing the Latter-day Saints, both here and else-where in the world. We hope that you will not be overcome with discouragement in your attempts to raise your families in righteousness. Remember that the Lord has commanded this: "But my dis-ciples shall stand in holy places, and shall not be moved" (D&C 45:32).
>
> While some interpret this to mean the temple, which surely it does, it also represents the homes in which we live. If you will diligently work to lead your families in righteousness, encouraging and participating in daily family prayer, scripture reading, family home evening, and love and sup-port for each other in living the teachings of the gospel, *you will receive the promised blessings of the Lord in raising a righteous posterity.*[15]

In an increasingly wicked world, how essential it is that each of us "stand in holy places" and commit to be true and faithful to the teachings of the gospel of Jesus Christ.

Notes

1. Gordon B. Hinckley, *Teachings of Gordon B. Hinckley* (Salt Lake City: Deseret Book, 1997), 207.

2. M. Russell Ballard, "Feasting at the Lord's Table," *Ensign*, May 1996, 81; emphasis added.

3. John H. Groberg, "The Power of Family Prayer," *Ensign*, May 1982, 50.

4. Jeffrey R. Holland, "A Prayer for the Children," *Ensign*, May 2003, 86.

5. A. Theodore Tuttle, "Therefore I Was Taught," *Ensign*, November 1979, 27.

6. The First Presidency, "Keeping Children Close to the Church," *Ensign*, June 1999, 80.

7. Boyd K. Packer, "Agency and Control," *Ensign*, May 1983, 67.

8. First Presidency, "Keeping Children Close to the Church," 80.

9. Harold B. Lee, *The Teachings of Harold B. Lee*, ed. Clyde J. Williams (Salt Lake City: Bookcraft, 1996), 264.

10. "Priesthood Correlation and the Home Evening," *Improvement Era*, December 1964, 1,079.

11. Spencer W. Kimball, *The Teachings of Spencer W. Kimball*, ed. Edward L. Kimball (Salt Lake City: Bookcraft, 1982), 344–45.

12. Ibid., 129; emphasis added.

13. Marion G. Romney, "The Book of Mormon," *Ensign*, May 1980, 67.

14. Jeffrey R. Holland, "A Prayer for the Children," 87.

15. Howard W. Hunter, *The Teachings of Howard W. Hunter*, ed. Clyde J. Williams (Salt Lake City: Bookcraft, 1997), 155; emphasis added.

Chapter 2

Lead Children to a Personal Relationship with God

A wise man once observed, "Our children are born *through* us, not *to* us." Although we may possess an eternal relationship with them—a sealing link that binds us together—our children are not our possessions. They do not belong to us in a material sense. They were our Heavenly Father's children long before they were ours. In a way, he has merely loaned them to us temporarily and given us the sacred responsibility to lead them back to him. Two familiar scriptural accounts, although not specifically about family relationships, serve to illustrate this important parenting principle.

The first comes from the ministry of John the Baptist. His foreordained mission was to be an Elias—one who prepares the way for someone even greater. He did not merely draw disciples to himself with his teachings, testimony, love, and devotion. Rather, because those who listened to him were inspired by his words and touched by his love, they accepted direction to their most important relationship—a relationship with the Savior of the world. John's message, as important and influential as it was, was merely a way station along the pathway to eternal life.

> Ye yourselves bear me witness, that I said, that I am not the Christ, but that I am sent before him. He that hath the bride is the bridegroom: but the friend of the bridegroom, which standeth and heareth him, rejoiceth greatly because of the bridegroom's voice: this my joy therefore is fulfilled. *He must increase, but I must decrease.* (John 3:28–30; emphasis added)

As parents, we must be like John—preparers of the way for our children to come to know the Master themselves. We can teach, love, nurture, strengthen, serve, and exemplify, but ultimately only the Savior can transform, forgive, secure, and save. Our homes are, so to speak, way stations in the eternal progression of our children. If they are to be righteous and responsible in a spiritually significant sense, if they are to have their own eternal companions and forever families, we must direct them to the one who can make these blessings possible and secure. We can point the way. We can teach them how to find him, but ultimately *we* must decrease so *he* can increase.

If we are to be successful at this, our influence must inevitably give way to the Savior's greater influence. Ironically, in guiding our children to their own personal relationship with God so that he can guide, direct, and comfort them, our influence in their lives becomes stronger and the love we have for each other increases.

The second scriptural account comes from Lehi's dream of the tree of life. We are familiar with the story and symbols of his dream: the iron rod, the strait and narrow path, the mists of darkness, the taunting and mocking of those in the great and spacious building, and the fruit of the tree, which "was desirable to make one happy" (1 Nephi 8:10). From Nephi's later commentary we learn the spiritual meaning of the symbolic elements of the dream. The iron rod is the word of God, the mists of darkness are the temptations of the devil, the great and spacious building represents the pride and wisdom of the world, and the fruit of the tree is the love of God as manifest through the atonement of Jesus Christ (1 Nephi 11–12).

Much has been written and spoken concerning this dream's meaning, message, and application. One particular application, drawn from observing what Lehi says and does *after* he arrives at the tree of life, applies to parents striving to rear righteous and responsible children:

> And it came to pass that I did go forth and partake of the fruit thereof; and I beheld that it was most sweet, above all that I ever before tasted. Yea, and I beheld that the fruit thereof was white, to exceed all the whiteness that I had ever seen.
>
> And as I partook of the fruit thereof it filled my soul with exceedingly great joy; wherefore, *I began to be desirous that my family should partake of it also;* for I knew that it was desirable above all other fruit.
>
> And as I cast my eyes round about, that perhaps I might discover my family also, I beheld a river of water; and it ran along, and it was near the tree of which I was partaking the fruit.
>
> And I looked to behold from whence it came; and I saw the head thereof a little way off; and at the head thereof I beheld your mother Sariah, and Sam, and Nephi; and they stood as if they knew not whither they should go.
>
> And it came to pass that I beckoned unto them; and I also did say unto them with a loud voice that they should come unto me, and partake of the fruit, which was desirable above all other fruit. (1 Nephi 8:11–15; emphasis added)

It may be as important for parents to note what Lehi didn't do, as well as what he did do. Any loving parent can relate to Lehi's desire that his family also partake of the love of Christ, which had infused his soul with unspeakable joy. Virtually every father would fuse desire with deeds, even extraordinary efforts, to ensure that his children partake of the fruit. Lehi also did all he could. However, he understood that there are some things parents cannot do.

We see Lehi exhorting his children "with all the feeling of a tender parent" (1 Nephi 8:37). What we don't see, however, is Lehi loading bushel baskets full of the fruit of the tree and carting them back to feed his family. We don't see him making applesauce from the fruit and mixing it with meals for Laman and Lemuel because they were unwilling to partake of the fruit themselves. We don't see Lehi force-feeding his children or providing some special shortcut through the mists of darkness to the tree. Each must come to the tree on his own. Each must cling to the iron rod and press forward against the mists of darkness. Each must ignore the mocking of those in the great and spacious building. Each must withstand the enticements to leave the strait and narrow path and join the wicked and worldly.

Lehi couldn't partake of the fruit *for* Laman and Lemuel. They had to do it for themselves. There is no other way to enjoy the fruits of the love of God.

A Firm Foundation of Personal Testimony

Just as Lehi desired that his family partake of the fruit of the tree, we desire that our children come to know for themselves the love of God. They do this as they come to know for themselves the truthfulness of the gospel, as they taste the sweet fruits of the companionship of the Holy Spirit, and as they experience, rather than just learn about, the blessings of the Atonement.

From our study and through years of observation and experience, we have learned that those youth who have partaken of the fruit of the tree by developing a spiritual relationship with God and by obtaining a personal testimony of the truths of the gospel are better equipped to repel the "fiery darts of the adversary" (1 Nephi 15:24). The "shield of faith" (Ephesians 6:16; D&C 27:17) that protects them and prompts them to make right choices has been produced *internally*. It is not something that can merely be applied *externally*. As President James E. Faust declared:

> Generally, those children who make the decision and have the resolve to abstain from drugs, alcohol, and illicit sex are those who have adopted and *internalized* the strong values of their homes as lived by their parents. In times of difficult decisions they are most likely to follow the teachings of their parents rather than the example of their peers or the sophistries of the media which glamorize alcohol consumption, illicit sex, infidelity, dishonesty, and other vices. . . .
>
> What seems to help cement parental [and Church] teachings and values in place in children's lives is a firm belief in Deity. *When this belief*

becomes part of their very souls, they have inner strength.[1]

Personal testimony and spirituality provide our children with a firm foundation upon which their lives can be securely built. It is the foundation of a house, not the *furnishings,* that gives it strength. Furnishings in the lives of our children—possessions, achievements, awards—will have little permanence or lasting meaning if the foundation is lacking. That foundation must be our Redeemer, a personal relationship with God, a testimony, and an internalization and application of gospel principles. This must be the rock solid foundation on which our children build their lives. Helaman declared to his sons:

> And now, my sons, remember, remember that it is upon the rock of our Redeemer, who is Christ, the Son of God, that ye must build your foundation; that when the devil shall send forth his mighty winds, yea, his shafts in the whirlwind, yea, when all his hail and mighty storm shall beat upon you, it shall have no power over you to drag you down to the gulf of misery and endless wo, because of the rock upon which ye are built, which is a sure foundation, a foundation whereon if men build they cannot fall. (Helaman 5:12)

All that we do as parents should point our children toward that desired end—the establishment of their own firm foundation of testimony. Everything we do with our religious endeavors at home *outwardly* should lead them to a personal witness of truth, which will motivate them *inwardly*. As one teen in our study said, "My parents' top priority was that we develop our own personal testimonies." Many other comments—both by way of positive experience and later regrets—from young people as well as from parents in our study testify of the foundational power of personal testimony:

A testimony of the Savior and of the gospel's truth is so necessary to resist temptation. In my eyes a testimony is the best prevention against Satan's temptations and is the most important thing parents can teach.

I wish I had gained my testimony earlier so that I would have been better able to overcome temptations and peer pressure. My testimony is now what gives me my strength.

We taught our children early on the importance of gaining their own testimony. We taught them not only what a testimony is but also how to get one. We often told our kids that they could come to know the truth about a principle that we were teaching them. They understood that we wanted them to know for themselves, not just rely on our testimonies.

We cannot obtain a personal testimony of the gospel or develop a personal relationship with God for our children, but there are certain things we *can* do that will help them build their own foundation.

Distinguish between Means and Ends

We have consistently found in our research that high religiosity of LDS teens is directly related to lower levels of delinquency, drug and alcohol use, immorality, and other illegal and dishonest behaviors. Yet there is an interesting twist to this no-brainer finding. Different dimensions of religiosity make up the religious character of Latter-day Saints. These include:

- Public religious behaviors, such as Church attendance and involvement in Church activities and programs.
- Professed religious beliefs, such as acceptance of the reality of God and a general belief in the doctrines and teachings of the Church.
- Private religious practices, such as personal prayer, scripture study, and fasting.
- Personal spirituality and spiritual experiences, such as feeling the Spirit, receiving answers to prayers, and making religion an important part of life.

All of these aspects of religiosity are important. We found, however, that in the lives of those young people who were most successful in resisting temptation and standing strong against negative peer pressure, one of these dimensions had a more profound impact than the others: personal spirituality. These young people had high levels of religiosity in the other areas, but things such as Church attendance, religious beliefs, and private religious practices had become a means to an end—personal testimony and spirituality.

Many youth, however, exhibit high levels of professed belief and may even regularly attend Church meetings and activities, yet they fail to live the standards or abide by the values espoused by the Church. There seems to be a major disconnect. Why? Perhaps the answer lies in the tendency for all of us to focus more on external behavior—such as attendance—than on internal conversion, which is difficult to observe and measure. In a way this can create a disconnect for parents as well if they are not careful.

For example, we want our daughters to obtain their Young Women medallion and our sons to achieve their Duty to God award. But is that the *end* we desire for them? Of course not! Do Church activity and achievement awards assure them of exaltation? Not necessarily, but they can be an important *means* to that *end*. External behaviors, no matter how noble and right they are, cannot guarantee salvation. Partaking of the fruit and tasting its sweetness require gospel internalization—personal spirituality, testimony, individual conversion, and endurance in righteousness.

We need to be as concerned about our children's

spiritual development, therefore, as we are about their Church attendance and involvement in activities and programs. All is not necessarily well in Zion just because we attend Church or talk about our lessons at Sunday dinner. All is not necessarily well at home just because we have regular family prayer and home evening. All is not necessarily well with our children just because they attend seminary, never miss a sacrament meeting, obtain their Young Men and Young Women achievement awards, and go to Especially for Youth. All of these things can be important helps along the way, but they aren't the end of the road.

We must not overlook the *ends* while we are working on the *means*. At the same time, we must remember that the *ends* are difficult, if not impossible, to attain without also availing ourselves and our children of the *means*. Perhaps one thought should guide us in all of our efforts to help our children partake of the "tree, whose fruit [is] desirable to make one happy" (1 Nephi 8:10). It is not enough to get our kids *into the Church*. We must get the gospel, a testimony, and the Spirit of the Lord *into them!*

The Importance of Personal Prayer and Scripture Study

If we were to identify one thing as the single most important factor in helping our children internalize gospel principles, gain a testimony, and develop spiritual strength to resist temptation, it would undoubtedly be personal prayer. It is the catalyst for the development of all other spiritual traits and strengths. There can be no individual testimony without it. Developing personal spirituality—feeling a closeness to God, viewing religion as important in daily life, and recognizing spiritual experiences—is impossible without prayer.

Those youth in our study who consistently and conscientiously prayed privately had significantly lower levels of inappropriate behaviors, including immorality and drug and alcohol use. They also exhibited greater strength to withstand negative peer pressure and temptation. In contrast, those young people who didn't live the standards of the Church and who engaged most frequently in delinquent behaviors, rarely, if ever, prayed privately. Ironically, however, even among this latter group, the majority reported that they participated regularly in family prayer.

As important as family prayer, family scripture study, and family home evening are, they are, nonetheless, *external* religious activities. Personal prayer and individual scripture study are *internal* religious behaviors that can have even greater power in the lives of our children.

If we are not careful, there can be an unintended downside to family prayer for both parents and children. Our children may get the idea that family prayer is all that counts because of our emphasis on its importance and our efforts to consistently hold it. We certainly don't want to give that message. Sometimes young people seem to think there is some sort of prayer quota. If you have family prayer, they reason, you don't need personal prayer—especially when you consider blessings on the food and prayers in seminary!

We want our children to be diligent in saying their prayers, but we may not explicitly give that message to them. Sometimes it takes so much effort to hold family prayer that we may figuratively (or sometimes literally) breathe a sigh of relief and think, "We did it!" Yes, we had family prayer, but we are not done praying, and neither are our children. The Savior taught that we should "pray always, that you may come off conqueror; yea, that you may conquer Satan, and that you may escape the hands of the servants of Satan that do uphold his work" (D&C 10:5).

We need to teach by personal example—saying our own prayers—and by explicit counsel that personal prayer is one of the most important protections against temptation. Daily personal prayer combined with regular family prayer becomes doubly powerful. President Ezra Taft Benson promised the youth of the Church, "If you will earnestly seek guidance from your Heavenly Father, morning and evening, *you will be given the strength to shun any temptation.*"[2]

Prophets and apostles have also urged all of us— young and old—to partake of the personal power that comes from daily reading the scriptures. Speaking specifically of the power of the Book of Mormon, President Benson declared:

> It is not just that the Book of Mormon teaches us truth, though it indeed does that. It is not just that the Book of Mormon bears testimony of Christ, though it indeed does that too. But there is something more. There is a power in the book which will begin to flow into your lives the moment you begin a serious study of the book. *You will find greater power to resist temptation. You will find the power to avoid deception.*[3]

What promises! Strength to shun any temptation, power to avoid deception! Our children need to understand, believe, and apply that prophetic counsel to realize those prophetic promises. We can help them do just that. Many of the young people in our study—teens and young adults alike—made insightful observations concerning the impact of their parents' efforts in this regard:

> My dad always reminds me, "Say your prayers." This reminds me that it is not enough to have family prayer: I must pray on my own.

I am so blessed now because my parents encouraged me when I was young to pray and read my scriptures on my own.

My parents encourage me to have faith and pray on my own so that I can have spiritual experiences for myself.

Perhaps the capstone statement that summarizes this important principle came from a response by a teenager to the question "What is the thing that helps you the most to live the gospel and resist temptation?" She replied, "Reading the scriptures and having personal prayer are things not to be done without!"

Provide Opportunities for Spiritual Experiences

For our children to develop a personal relationship with God and obtain their own testimony of the truthfulness of the gospel, they need to feel the spirit of the Lord in their lives. That is what we hope for them. One of the means to that end is to provide our children with opportunities for spiritual experiences. Note that we can *only provide the opportunities*, not the actual spiritual experiences. Those come from the Lord on his terms and timetable, not ours. The influence of the Spirit cannot be contrived or manipulated.

All we can do is provide our children with

experiences that are conducive to the Spirit and pray that their hearts will be touched. Within the context of the family, our children learn best about the gospel, see it in action, and experience the fruits of gospel living.

A father of teenagers reported that he was grumbling to his wife about the apparent lack of Church-sponsored service projects and meaningful activities designed for the spiritual development of the youth in the ward. His wife's response caused him to rethink his role as the patriarch of their family.

"Why do we have to wait for the Church to provide our children with meaningful service projects and spiritual activities?" she asked. "Why can't we provide them as a family?" He reported:

> Her words hit me right between the eyes. I realized that I had been expecting the programs of the Church to do my job for me. I want my children to be instructed and feel the Spirit by their involvement in the Church, but that is somewhat out of my control. I can control, however, what we do in our home and as a family. From that moment I have tried to provide more opportunities for my children to serve God and their fellowmen in some manner, and in turn, feel the Spirit in their lives. Those family-generated experiences have been some of the most meaningful things we have done. I have learned that Church activities are there to help us as a family, but they cannot replace the family. Spiritual experiences

that come within the family context can have even greater power than what the ward can do.

Many young people in our study talked about special family moments—many of which were spontaneous and unexpected—when they felt an outpouring of the Spirit. One young woman told of an experience in which her family went to the temple and did baptisms for the dead for some of their ancestors. Afterward, she said her parents talked to the children about the importance of the temple.

"They told us how much they loved the temple and how thankful they were to have us sealed to them," she remembered. "We had heard these things before, but because of what we had just been doing as a family, their testimonies had a powerful impact on us."

Others reported strong spiritual feelings that came to them as they received father's blessings or witnessed the blessing of a sick family member, fasted for someone with special needs, or held impromptu testimony meetings. Sometimes simple things yielded the most profound spiritual feelings.

"One of the best spiritual experiences of my life has been just singing hymns together at the piano," one young woman remembered. A young adult man recalled, "Our family often did service for other people. This helped me internalize the gospel because I could see the good we were doing for others, and I realized how blessed we really were."

Even sitting around the dinner table on Sundays can be an opportunity for spiritual experiences. "We talked about what we had learned in Church," one young man said. "Mom and Dad would also share what they had learned and would bear their testimonies and share their feelings. This may seem simple, but it really had an influence on me."

Encourage Children to Know for Themselves

"I am satisfied . . . that whenever a man has a true witness in his heart of the living reality of the Lord Jesus Christ *all else will come together as it should* . . . ," President Gordon B. Hinckley said. "That is the root from which all virtue springs among those who call themselves Latter-day Saints."[4]

Our research, combined with our many years of leadership in the Church, confirms President Hinckley's testimony. Those young people who have gained their own personal witness of the divinity of the Savior and the truthfulness of the gospel have fewer behavioral problems and greater strength to resist temptation and negative peer pressure.

Virtually all of the youth in our study (97 percent) expressed a strong belief in the gospel and the Savior's mission as the redeemer of the world. Yet many of those who professed such beliefs still engaged in immoral, dishonest, delinquent, or illegal behaviors. On the other hand, among those youth who internalized the gospel, felt a closeness to God in their lives, and had received their own personal testimony by the power of the Holy Ghost, relatively few engaged in those behaviors.

When youth come to know for themselves, rather than merely accept and rely on the testimonies of parents, leaders, and teachers, they have spiritual power. The sooner we can help them to know for themselves, the better. The comments of many of the young people we have surveyed through the years provide a powerful witness to that fact:

> Looking back now, I wish I had tried to gain a stronger testimony earlier than I did. It would have given me more strength to rely on.

> I wish I had developed a strong testimony early in life. I found by the time I had strengthened my testimony or experienced my personal conversion, I had already given in to many temptations which I regret to this day. I wish I had not acted "too cool" for the gospel and instead softened my heart so a testimony could have entered it.

It is probably not coincidental that the first questions asked as part of a temple recommend interview—before any examination concerning worthy behavior—deal with issues of personal testimony. If our children have a burning testimony, worthy behavior will follow. So we need to do more than merely monitor their behavior; we need to nurture the development of their testimonies. We do that by teaching them the doctrines of the gospel, the standards of worthy behavior, the importance of gaining a personal testimony, and how to gain that testimony.

Those of us who have helped children learn to ride a bike understand this principle. As they first attempt to ride, we are there to hold them up, support them, and sometimes kiss away the "owies" when they fall. Neither they nor we will be satisfied if we hold them up the rest of their lives. We can lessen their need for our support and presence by providing training wheels. But if they are ever going to find the enjoyment that comes with bike riding, the training wheels must eventually come off.

For our children to develop their own testimonies, we must teach them, love them, support them, and encourage them, even as we allow them to rely on spiritual training wheels—our testimonies. But we must encourage them to take off the training wheels as soon as they can and stand on the power of their own testimonies.

In past generations, it may have been possible for children and parents alike to spiritually glide through life as "cultural converts" or "social Saints" and remain relatively unburned by the adversary's fiery darts. In this day and age, however, it is virtually impossible. As the spiritual conditions of modern society deteriorate, the middle ground grows narrow. Personal testimony and spiritual conversion provide our greatest earthly protection.

Because Satan targets our children at younger and younger ages, they must obtain a meaningful relationship with God and develop a testimony of the truthfulness of the gospel sooner rather than later. It's never too early, but it can become too late. We may be seeing the fulfillment of a prophecy uttered by President Heber C. Kimball in the mid-nineteenth century. His warning should echo in our ears and burn in our hearts as we daily strive to lead our children to God:

> To meet the difficulties that are coming, it will be necessary for you to have a knowledge of the truth of this work for yourselves. The difficulties will be of such a character that the man or woman [or youth] who does not possess this personal knowledge or witness will fall. . . . The time will come when no man nor woman will be able to endure on borrowed light. Each will have to be guided by the light within himself. If you do not have it, how can you stand?[5]

Notes

1. James E. Faust, "The Greatest Challenge in the World—Good Parenting," *Ensign,* November 1990, 34; emphasis added.

2. Ezra Taft Benson, "A Message to the Rising Generation," *Ensign,* November 1977, 32; emphasis added.

    3. Ezra Taft Benson, *The Teachings of Ezra Taft Benson* (Salt Lake City: Bookcraft, 1988), 54; emphasis added.
    4. Gordon B. Hinckley, *Teachings of Gordon B. Hinckley* (Salt Lake City: Deseret Book, 1997), 648; emphasis added.
    5. Orson F. Whitney, *Life of Heber C. Kimball*, 3d ed. (Salt Lake City: Bookcraft, 1967), 450.

Chapter 3

Render Daily Outpourings
of Love

Gardeners know it is vitally important to properly prepare soil and plant quality seeds. Proper amounts of moisture, fertilizer, and sunlight are also required, and continual effort must be given to weeding and controlling pests. But as important as these steps are, plants will not grow and yield a bounteous harvest without adequate warmth.

The importance of a warm growing environment is easily seen in wintertime. The soil is virtually the same. The sun may even be shining brightly. But without warmth, the seeds—no matter how good they are—will never germinate or grow. Even after the soil warms enough in the spring to provide a proper growing environment, tender plants can be harmed or destroyed by a cold spell. We use the term *killing frost* to describe such an event. All of these conditions—a warm growing environment, a cold spell, a killing frost, and everything inbetween—can also be found in homes and families.

The principles are much the same for "growing" healthy, happy, and productive children. Cold spells and killing frosts, emotionally speaking, can be just as damaging to children as they are to plants. In fact, the consequences of a killing frost in a family may be worse and its implications longer-lasting. The good seeds of gospel teaching sown within a family, like the seeds sown in a garden, can only germinate, take root, and thrive in an emotionally warm environment. Faith is fortified by love. Testimony is nurtured with affection. Spirituality is developed in a warm environment of emotional closeness between parents and children.

Warmth is as necessary for humans as it is for plants. Seeds of faith—sown by gospel instruction at home, family prayer, and family scripture study—will not produce the fruit we desire in the lives of our children if the temperature of our home environment—the emotional warmth of our homes—is insufficient.

Creating a home environment where children learn the gospel, live its precepts, love the Lord, and are unified with and obedient to parents requires liberal outpourings of love every day. We prove our love with every action and every word. Loving our children requires that we tell them and show them.

"It's about Time"

Money has value. But its value is not found in the metallic content of a coin or the printed paper of a bill but rather in what it represents and what it is able to do for us. To a small child, a dime or nickel doesn't have much intrinsic value, but the piece of bubble gum that the coin can be exchanged for does. Money is a tangible commodity representing our work and effort.

Time is the currency of love. It is a commodity that represents our love. It is difficult to precisely define love, but it is quite easy to describe how to show love. The phrase "I love you"—as important as it is—is somewhat abstract to a child. He may know in a superficial way what the words mean. But what really matters is that his father plays ball with him or that his mother reads to him. The time a parent spends with a child is a very real commodity of value, a tangible evidence of love.

In recent years Church Public Affairs has produced a popular advertising campaign for television and radio known as the "Homefront" series. The campaign's vignettes highlight clever, thought-provoking ways that parents can better show their love by giving time to their children. The spots end with either, "Give your children everything—give them your time" or "Family. Isn't it about time?" Time with, and the attention of, parents is the commodity of love that children most understand and appreciate. Gifts such as toys are but substitutes for the real evidence of our love—our most precious earthly commodity—our time. In this way, giving our time is truly giving everything.

Much has been said about *quality time* versus *quantity time.* It is a discussion that only adults and busy parents have. Children usually don't make distinctions. To them, quantity time *is* quality time. There can be no quality without a considerable measure of quantity. To think that sporadic, intense interaction can make up for long periods of limited personal contact or even neglect is ludicrous.

Our children are intuitive enough to know that true quality time involves not only quantity but also affection and emotional closeness. To believe otherwise is as silly as the home teacher who excuses his inattention to duty by saying, "I have quality visits. I may only see my families once a year, but my visits are really good." Too often the quality time argument is nothing but a feeble justification for giving less time and attention than we should to those we love. President James E. Faust said:

> One of the main problems in society today is that we spend less and less time together. Some, even when they are together, spend an extraordinary amount of time in front of the television,

which robs them of personal time for reinforcing feelings of self-worth. . . . Time together is precious—time needed to encourage and to show how to do things. Less time together can result in loneliness, which may produce feelings of being unsupported, untreasured, and inadequate.[1]

Successfully raising a family and creating a loving, emotionally connected home takes a lot of time, regardless of our station in life, our respective responsibilities, and the demands placed upon us. There are no shortcuts. As one author wrote, "Kids don't do meetings. You can't raise them in short, scheduled bursts. They need lots of attention."[2]

We know from experience and observation that today's parents are busy—perhaps stressed and stretched more than any previous generation. As children grow older and become more involved in their own activities, they too become busy. That is all the more reason that time—the amount as well as the intensity—must be our most valuable currency of love. What can we do, especially amidst the frantic and hurry-scurry climate of modern society, to spend more time—both quality and quantity—together as families? From the thousands of youth, young adults, and experienced parents we have studied through the years, a few family practices have emerged as important means whereby time invested yields rich dividends.

Have Fun Together

The old adage "All work and no play makes Jack a dull boy" applies to families as well as to individuals. Family closeness and emotional connectedness can be strengthened through playing and laughing together. Sometimes even activities that by their very nature aren't intended to be fun, like doing dishes, cleaning the house, or working in the yard, can be productive in emotional ways. Sometimes children work and serve better when the time is punctuated with "fun breaks" or "ice cream rewards."

Family fun can be experienced with both planned and unplanned activities. But just because something is unplanned doesn't mean it requires no effort. The fun—the laughter, the bonding, the time shared together—may be spontaneous, but the event itself has to come from a commitment to putting family first. One teenager's comment illustrates this kind of commitment, especially when parents are busy: "Even though my dad is a very busy man, he tries to attend my (and the other kids') activities and always makes time for us to do things together as a family."

Whether it be simple things like playing catch in the backyard, riding bikes, holding spontaneous pillow fights, or doing more elaborate activities such as family vacations, opportunities for family fun are abundant. Excuses like "I don't have time" or "We can't afford it" are generally just that—excuses for our lack of commitment. We all have the same amount of time every day, and having fun together doesn't need to cost anything. We just need to open our eyes and hearts, make time, and show our love to our children by our willingness to "give them everything"—our precious time and attention.

There seems to be little correlation between the amount of money spent on exotic adventures or exciting toys and the lasting memories our children have of home and family. Often simple, sometimes even silly, things are fondly retained in the hearts and memories of our family members long after the expensive toys are broken and forgotten or the souvenirs from the family cruise in the Caribbean are discarded. One young woman remembered:

> Our family had lots of fun activities and vacations. But I must admit the thing that I remember most was the family "campout" in our backyard. At first I was embarrassed because it seemed ridiculous, but it was so fun. We cooked on a camp stove, ate on a picnic table, sang campfire songs around the propane lantern, and slept in the tent that Dad and my brother put up. There was a lot of laughter. The neighbors probably thought we were crazy, but that is what made it so fun. I can't remember all of our vacations, but I'll never forget this "campout."

When we asked what was the most important or effective thing they did (or are doing) to rear their children, the experienced parents in our study responded that it was showing love through spending time and having fun together:

> I read to my children every night. This may seem overly simplistic, but it was very important. It was a great bonding time. It was made especially fun when we made up our own "sound effects" for the stories.

> The one thing that probably saved us as a family was that we played together. We really made a point of having fun and included the nice friends of our children.

> We spend a lot of time together. Our children know that we would rather be with them than anyone else.

In contrast, many young people (as well some parents) lamented the fact that they didn't spend much time or have much fun together as a family. This was often perceived, however erroneously, as a lack of love and devotion. Children whose parents won't "chill out" and have fun often feel estranged. "I wish my parents would lighten up a little and have fun," one young man said. "They are so serious all the time; it makes me think they are mad at me."

Develop Family Traditions

One of the most important ways we can demonstrate our emotional connectedness, loyalty, and love as a family is through appropriate family traditions. Special events such as holidays, birthdays, Church ordinances, graduations, and other important events provide us with an opportunity to create memorable family traditions. Sometimes these traditions may begin somewhat accidentally, but over time they become perpetuated and planned.

Interestingly, even as teenagers seek to exert independence from their parents and family, they feel a special connection through traditions. Once traditions are established, children often are the ones who ensure that they continue. For example, one father reported that a tradition associated with watching general conference on television together as family began more "out of desperation than inspiration":

> When our boys were little, to help keep them occupied as we watched general conference we would all sit on the floor and listen as we built things with Lincoln Logs. From that point on, every six months we could be found on the family room floor playing with building blocks and listening to conference talks. When the boys became teenagers they insisted that we bring out the Lincoln Logs or Lego blocks as we watched conference together. They will probably do the same thing with their kids.

Many of the young people we surveyed spoke of traditions associated with their birthdays that made them feel special and loved. "On my birthday, even as I got older," one young adult remembered, "my parents always went to great lengths to make it a special and fun day for me." Others spoke of being able to choose what the family would eat on their birthday, including going grocery shopping with their mothers to buy the necessary ingredients for their birthday dinner. It became a special tradition, unique to each child.

Some youth mentioned a birthday tradition of going out to dinner alone with their parents. In some families, girls got to go on a special birthday daddy-daughter date, and sons practiced their social skills at a dinner date with Mom. One teenage girl reported, "We can go wherever we want. It used to be McDonald's when I was little, but now it's Olive Garden."

Another oft-reported family tradition is back-to-school father's blessings. A back-to-school blessing can be a spiritually strengthening experience as well as a time of emotional bonding and family loyalty. Each child, in addition to receiving a unique blessing of comfort and guidance, will feel affection and love. One father stated, "My children may think that hugging is actually part of the ordinance because I tell them (somewhat jokingly) that the blessing won't work unless it is sealed with a hug."

During our service as bishops, many young people told us that they never, or rarely, received father's blessings, even though most of them had fathers who were active and worthy priesthood holders. When we counseled these young people to ask their fathers for a blessing, some of them responded with a look that said, "You mean I can do that?" The results were amazing. Almost to a man, the fathers were honored and gratified that their children desired a blessing at their hands. The result was spiritual strength for the one blessed and an increased emotional closeness between fathers and families. A special power—spiritual and emotional—attends blessings. Fathers may never know in mortality how much their children appreciate these blessings and how much the blessings helped them in their struggles and challenges.

Spend Time with Each Child

Our children need, desire, and appreciate one-on-one time with their parents. Time spent with individual children shows even greater commitment to family by demonstrating parental love for one child at a time, not just the family unit as a whole. This is particularly important in the Latter-day Saint culture, where families tend to be larger than average. Large families make it more difficult, but it's all the more important that parents spend time talking, playing, and interacting with each child independent of the others. Several comments from young people illustrate this.

"I wish my parents would listen to me on an

individual basis more," one teenager in our study lamented. "Five to ten minutes of individual one-on-one time makes a big difference." Another stated, "There are eight kids in our family. Although I know it would be hard, I wish we could have more one-on-one time with our parents."

Children are unique individuals with unique needs, and they are raised one at a time. The reality of this fact hits us between the eyes when we realize that what had worked so well with one child doesn't work at all on another child. We wonder if this is evidence of God's sense of humor, reminding us that our children are individuals—even though they come from the same family and may resemble each other or us, their parents.

Several comments from both youth and parents provide ideas on showing greater love for each child: "When I was real young (elementary school), my mother had 'days' for each of her kids every month," one young adult remembered. "It was our special day to be with Mom and do things just with her."

In a similar vein, one teenage boy reported that as he and his siblings were growing up they shared occasional "special nights" with their parents, staying up late with Mom and Dad "without all the other kids around." One father reported that whenever he has an errand to do, such as run to the hardware store, he takes one of his children with him.

Another remembered that when he came home from work each day, he would invite one of his children to accompany him to the convenience store to get a drink or a treat. For his children, the real treat was spending time with their dad. Truly, a major expression of love is being willing to give time—both *quality* and *quantity*—to each of our children. This tells them we value them as individuals and as important members of the family.

A Hug a Day Keeps Many Problems Away

We also show love for our children with appropriate gestures of physical affection. A hug, a kiss on the cheek, a touch on the arm, or an arm around a shoulder can say "I love you" in important ways. For some parents and children, expressions of physical affection can be uncomfortable, but such expressions are important and should not be minimized or neglected.

It is easy for parents to show physical affection to babies, toddlers, and small children. But for many parents, the older and bigger their children become, the less they hug and kiss them. In some ways this is normal and appropriate, but we must never think that our children outgrow the need to feel our loving hugs and kisses. One experienced mother recalled, "I was affectionate with my boys when they were small, but when they began to pull away, I thought I should respect their feelings and stop physical demonstrations of affection. Now I regret it and wish I had not done so."

When our children become adolescents, regardless of their tough-guy exteriors, they may need affection just as much, if not more, than they did as toddlers. "My family is not a hugging, touchy-feely family," wrote one teenage girl in our study. "I can count on one hand the number of times I've hugged my brother. Each time is vividly remembered and very important to me. I wish we would show our love more openly."

Research shows that young women who have been deprived of physical affection from their parents, particularly their fathers, often resort to premarital sex in order to feel physical acceptance and affection. It is equally important that our sons receive hugs and kisses from both parents. Our research shows a direct relationship between those youth who feel affection from their parents and their ability to withstand the temptations of immorality.

Certainly, they may recoil and feign disgust because expressing familial affection may not seem like the grown-up thing to do, but it has a positive impact on them. They like it and appreciate it even if they make you feel that you're hugging a porcupine. One young adult man proudly declared, "Even though I am a returned missionary and live on my own, my mom still kisses me and tells me that she loves me whenever I see her."

What a contrast to the many comments we received from teens who lamented that their parents never hugged or kissed them. Perhaps we should view hugs and kisses like daily vitamins. You can live without them for a while, but you won't feel as well. Eventually, emotional malnourishment will take its toll. In a real sense, a hug a day keeps many problems away.

"I Love You"

In the famous Broadway musical and Hollywood motion picture *Fiddler on the Roof*, Tevye, the main character, asks his wife, "Golda, do you love me?" She responds, "Do I what?" Tevye persists, "Do you love me?" The scene that follows demonstrates the need for both words and deeds in expressing our love.

Golda recounts in song all of the things she has done for Tevye through their decades of marriage: cooking his meals, darning his socks, bearing his children. "But do you love me?" Tevye asks again. He doesn't question her devotion or love as seen in the myriad deeds she has done. His question really bespeaks a desire to hear the words "I love you."

Each of us, including our children, needs to hear verbal assurances of love, even when we see active evidence of it. Both kinds of love—words and deeds—are essential to a happy family. The deeds that show our love, such as giving time and attention, are like sunshine, soil, and water for tender plants. Sincere verbal expressions of love, such as "I love you," "I am proud of you," "I am thankful for you," and "You mean so much to me," are like fertilizer—emotional nutrients that stimulate good growth and deep roots.

The importance of such verbal expressions can be seen in many of the comments from the youth in our study—comments that celebrated the abundance of verbal expressions of love within the home or lamented their lack:

> My parents tell me more than three times a day that they love me. We never leave home or hang up the phone without saying, "I love you."

> When I come home at night I always tell my parents, "Good night" and "I love you." They always say it back.

> There are few "I love you's" in our family. As a result, it makes me feel uncomfortable to say it because expressions of love just don't exist in our home.

> I wish my parents had told me that they love me more. In my house, such emotions are looked down upon, and we have problems expressing love to each other.

> I can't recall ever being hugged, kissed, or told "I love you" after the age of five. Of course, I am not very good at showing affection either.

It is sad that any child, particularly any child raised in a Latter-day Saint home, could count on one hand the number of times she has heard "I love you" expressed by her parents. At times it may be difficult for us to verbally express love for our children (especially when we may not feel love toward them), but we must overcome that difficulty. Children may need words of loving reassurance the most when they are the least loveable. And they may pretend that they don't want to hear "I love you," but deep inside they will appreciate the words and the feeling of security that accompanies them. One father recalled how difficult it was for him to express his love to a challenging child who regularly rebuffed his efforts:

> I sort of had to trick him with my expressions of love. I would call out his full name in a stern voice. To which my son would answer, assuming he was in some kind of trouble, "What?" I would answer matter-of-factly, "I love you!" To which he would roll his eyes and say, "Whatever," and walk away, trying to hide the smile on his face.

In addition to the words "I love you," our children need to hear another phrase from us. It is also an expression of love and respect and is sometimes harder to say than "I love you." This phrase is "I'm sorry."

None of us is a perfect parent. Sometimes we make mistakes—more often than we like to. Our children are keenly aware of this. Yet they are usually pretty forgiving and compassionate if we are willing to sincerely apologize when we fall short. Saying "I'm sorry" can be a powerful expression of love and affection. In fact, in contrast to the dumb line from the 1970s motion picture *Love Story*—"Love means never having to say you're sorry"—real love means *always* being willing to apologize.

Regarding parental expressions of love—giving time, showing physical affection, expressing love verbally—the results of our research are both encouraging and somewhat discouraging. Nearly three-fourths of the youth we surveyed stated that their mothers are good at expressing love and affection. But only about half said their fathers are good at it. Likewise, nearly two-thirds of the youth said their mothers show them a great deal of attention. Fathers, however, show significantly less attention to and spend considerably less time doing things with their children.

These results are understandable, given that fathers generally work outside the home in greater numbers than do mothers. That does not, however, excuse fathers. The responsibilities of work and Church service, which many mothers also share, may make it challenging for fathers to spend time with their children. But responsibilities should never stop fathers from rendering daily portions of love in word and in deed. One father, whose children are now raised, lamented that his priorities had been out of order when he was younger:

> I was too self-absorbed with the role of provider and Church leader. I didn't spend as much time with my children, and I wasn't as involved in their upbringing as I should have been. I placed too much of the home-life responsibility on my wife, while I was too focused on matters outside our home.

In contrast, one of the teens in our study gave a glowing report on how her father balanced the demands of life:

> Although my dad is a doctor and is very busy, we always know that the family is more important to him than his job. He always wants to do things together as a family when he is home. I am especially grateful for the individual time we have with him. He takes the girls on daddy-daughter dates and goes camping and fishing with the boys. We also have time each month for personal interviews with Dad.

Another young person spoke of the value of father's interviews.

> My father sets aside time each month for father's interviews. It is a time to focus on me and me only. I can talk about anything I want to for as long as I want. It means a lot to me to be able to have deep, quality conversations with my father.

Fathers have a sacred responsibility to their children—a responsibility that cannot be shirked in the name of employment or Church work. A healthy family requires a proper balance of the temporal and the spiritual. Providing for a family means much more than putting food on the table, buying school clothes, and paying the mortgage.

Different Strokes for Different Folks

Like individuals, families have unique personalities and styles. Some families are reserved and quiet. Others are gregarious and loud. Just because a father doesn't enjoy camping doesn't make him a bad father. Just because a mother doesn't kiss her children on the lips doesn't make her a bad mother. Parents from different families simply have different ways of expressing love and spending time with their children.

It isn't so much a matter of *how* we express love as it is that we *do* express love. Our children don't expect us to be something we're not or to act in ways that would be unnatural for us. They do, however, need to know that we love them. They appreciate any effort on our part to show them, especially when they know it may be difficult for us. Several comments from the young people we surveyed illustrate this appreciation:

Many young boys grow up with fathers that take them camping, fishing, and hunting. My dad only did those things when there was no way around it. Even though he didn't like camping, he took me on the fathers and sons' campout every year. I know it was hard for him, but I appreciated it because it showed me how much he loved me and cared about me. Even though he didn't like camping, he always found other ways to show his love and spend time with me.

My mother came from a home where there was little expression of love and less hugging and kissing. She wasn't comfortable with such expressions, yet she would still give us a hug when we did something special and tell us that she loved us. It probably took a lot to be able to do that. Because it was hard for her, I was always deeply touched when she hugged me and told me she loved me.

My father knows nothing about computers. He is a jock, and I am a geek. I don't like sports, but I know he still loves me. When he plays computer games with me or talks to me about what I am working on, it means a lot to me.

The old adage "different strokes for different folks" certainly applies to the broad spectrum of parenting styles, even within the Church. We must not, however, allow excuses or personal discomfort to stop us from taking advantage of opportunities to draw our children close with expressions of love. Giving of our time when we are busy, being involved in an activity we may not enjoy, hugging, or saying "I love you" will have a great impact in the lives of our children and yield enduring returns.

Love Your Spouse

Expressions of love between husband and wife are also important expressions of love for children. Every loving word, act of kindness, and gesture of affection between husband and wife contributes to children's sense of security and love in the home. Love spoken and tenderness shown by parents to each other sets the stage for such expressions to be conveyed to children. "Because I see the incredible love my parents have for each other," one teenage girl observed, "I know how much I am loved."

Unfortunately, not all children are so blessed. Many are left to wonder if they are loved, despite the best efforts of their parents, because of the lack of love and devotion their parents show each other. Tension between parents creates tension within children.

"I wish my parents could have loved each other more as I was growing up," one young adult said. "No matter how much they said they loved and respected me, because of the lack of love and respect they had for each other, it hurt me and my relationship with them."

As we strive to show our children how much we love them, let us remember that the foundation of a happy family is built upon a loving, happy marriage.

Strengthening our marriage shows love for our children. "One of the greatest things a father can do for his children is to love their mother," taught President Howard W. Hunter.[3] Certainly the same applies to mothers.

Love Is the Great Motivator

Expressing love to our children in ways mentioned in this chapter will affect not only our home environment and the happiness of our families but also how our children will live their lives. One young person said:

> I feel so much love for my parents that I desire to please them. So not only do I not want to do "bad" things because I have been taught that they are wrong but also because I love and respect my parents so much. I don't want to disappoint them. To me, disappointing my parents would be almost worse than actually doing "bad" things because I love them and they love me so much. I don't ever want to break their trust.

Love is the great motivator. It is what activates all gospel instruction received at home and at Church. It is what gives reason and meaning to family rules, discipline, and expectations of obedience. It is the catalyst for righteousness. President Joseph F. Smith taught the power of parental love:

> If you will keep your [children] close to your heart, within the clasp of your arms; if you will

make them . . . feel you love them . . . and keep them near you, they will not go very far from you, and they will not commit any very great sin. . . .

If you wish your children to be taught in the principles of the gospel, if you wish them to love truth and understand it, if you wish them to be obedient to and united with you, love them! And prove . . . that you do love them by your every word or act to[ward] them.[4]

Notes

1. James E. Faust, "Enriching Our Lives through Family Home Evening," *Ensign,* June 2003, 5.

2. Laura Shapiro, "The Myth of Quality Time," *Newsweek,* 12 May 1997, 62.

3. *The Teachings of Howard W. Hunter,* ed. Clyde J. Williams (Salt Lake City: Bookcraft, 1997), 152.

4. Joseph F. Smith, *Gospel Doctrine,* ed. Joseph Fielding Smith, 5th ed. (Salt Lake City: Deseret Book, 1966), 316.

Chapter 4

Focus on Friends

♥

When Judith Rich Harris's book *The Nurture Assumption* became a runaway best-seller, many parents threw up their hands in frustration and abdicated their parental responsibilities out of a sense of helplessness and hopelessness. Harris rather convincingly argued that parents are largely irrelevant in their children's lives. According to her thesis, peers, not parents, determine whether children do well in school, go to college, become involved in delinquent behavior, use drugs and alcohol, engage in premarital sex, and so on. Parents can neither be blamed for their children's misbehavior nor receive credit for their achievements or successes. Generally speaking, parents neither help nor harm.

Harris's ideas were widely applauded on talk

shows as she absolved parents from the responsibility of raising their children. In good conscience, a
father can skip his son's soccer game to go golfing
on Saturday morning because watching his son play
makes no difference in his teenager's life. A mother
can go shopping rather than attend a parent-teacher
conference because the latter is irrelevant in how
well her teen does in school. No wonder so many
mothers and fathers embraced this approach to
parenting.

To Latter-day Saint parents, this would mean that
nothing we do—teaching the gospel, loving, praying, disciplining—would have any influence on our
children living the gospel, being active in the
Church, serving missions, marrying in the temple,
and leading righteous and responsible lives. Only
their friends would have an influence on them. What
nonsense! If this were true, you would see the
prophets and apostles advocating friends as the
basic unit of society and issuing a solemn proclamation on peers, not on the everlasting family.

The results of our research—both the scientific,
statistical results and the anecdotal comments of
youth—reveal the profound impact parents have on
their children's lives. Our studies overwhelmingly
demonstrate that parental influence is linked to academic achievement, self-esteem, and behavior
among Latter-day Saint youth. Generally speaking,
teens behave as they have been taught by their
parents. Whether by conscientious teaching in the

home or by daily example, parents do make a difference—an inestimable difference!

Parents should never underestimate their continuing influence in the lives of their children. That vital influence neither begins nor ends with the teenage years. Nevertheless, peers do exercise a dynamic influence in the lives of our children, particularly adolescents. Teens seek self-reliance and independence. This leads them to increasingly interact with and be influenced by their peers.

In the pages that follow, we will share some insights into the power peers have in the lives of LDS youth and offer suggestions on how we can maximize the positive influence of our children's good friends and minimize the impact of their bad friends. These principles are important, whether our children are in grade school or grad school.

The Power of Peers

Over the past several decades, social scientists have conducted hundreds of studies that demonstrate the power of peers in predicting delinquent behavior. For example, "Differential Association Theory," a sociological theory that has been around a long time, explains how delinquent friends influence a teenager to become involved in illegal or immoral behavior.

According to this theory, if your teenager has ten close friends and all ten smoke marijuana, the probability is high—in fact almost certain—that your son or daughter will become involved in marijuana use. On the other hand, if all ten close friends do not smoke marijuana, your son or daughter most likely will avoid it as well. If half of the friends smoke and half do not, your teenager is at risk but may escape marijuana use.

Marijuana-smoking friends do more than just exert overt, external pressure on our teens. These so-called friends also share values and beliefs that support drug use. Peers provide a powerful social network that exerts an influence above and beyond mere in-your-face peer pressure. For this reason, peer influences can come as much by the example—behavior and attitudes—of friends as by their direct, verbal pressure on our children to engage in certain activities.

Powerful, empirical support for Differential Association Theory should not discourage us. Just as delinquent friends can have a negative influence, friends who are committed to academic excellence, personal virtue, faith in God, and involvement in Church activity can influence our teenagers for good. Our greatest challenge is to guide our children toward friends who will have a positive influence on their lives and away from those who won't.

We asked the youth in our studies what had helped them to keep the commandments and stay active in the Church and what had influenced them to disobey the commandments and drift into inactivity. We were surprised that the most frequent answer to both questions was "my friends." Responses illustrate how friends can be either a righteous influence for good or an unrighteous influence for bad:

My LDS friends helped me stay true and my non-LDS friends pressured me to do bad things like drinking, using drugs, and having sex.

It is difficult being an LDS youth in the British Isles because here everyone at least drinks and has premarital sex. The Church is hardly known about to non-LDS youth. In fact, I'm seen as "weird" because I don't do those things that are the social norms for young people. Strong friends at Church help me keep the standards.

The strongest influence in my life to live the standards of the gospel has definitely been Church friends. Life really is harder in non-LDS communities. I personally feel everyone outside the Church is trying to tempt me to drink and smoke. I'll never give in, but it is really very difficult. This is why I'm trying to go to as many Church activities as possible, even if I know I won't like them. I will go to associate with true friends who keep me strong in the gospel.

The strongest influence in my life has been my so-called friends from school. I did wrong by following them because now I'm in college doing retakes in math and English. My friends interfered with the grades I needed. I felt that if I had not taken drugs, I wouldn't have been popular. Now I'm in college, and I can't stop smoking. If I hadn't followed my friends at school, I wouldn't be where I am now.

"My Friends Don't Influence Me"

Perhaps every parent, at some time or another, has heard this comment: "My friends don't influence me." Young people may actually believe they can play with fire and not get burned, that they can "hang out" with bad friends without following their example. The rationale for this argument is the same as saying, "I can watch bad videos and listen to bad music without being affected by it." The youth who believes this assumes that no influence exists in the absence of blatant pressure to engage in immoral behavior.

Such a view flies in the face of the multibillion-dollar advertising industry. Advertising banks on the fact that people, no matter how strong or weak their willpower, will act in certain ways because of continual exposure to enticing stimuli and subliminal messages. Advertising influences all of us—whether we admit it or not.

Likewise, our children are influenced over time by exposure to the attitudes and actions of their peers. Young people simply cannot have friends without being influenced by them. All of us, young and old alike, are influenced for good or bad by the people and messages that surround us.

Our research demonstrates that LDS youth whose closest friends engage in dishonesty, immorality, or drug abuse are several times more likely to become involved in such activities than LDS youth whose friends aren't involved in those things. This holds true even if their friends don't pressure them to engage in inappropriate behavior with statements such as "I dare you," "Be cool," "Are you chicken?" or "If you really love me, you will do this." One young adult woman remembered:

> When I was a teenager I never would admit it, but now I can see that my friends had a negative influence on me more than I thought. I thought I was strong and that my "wild" friends wouldn't affect me. I was strong and stood up against their teasings and temptings, but in my efforts to "save" them I can see that over time I started to compromise my standards and accept things that weren't right. Hanging out with bad friends will affect you even if you think it won't.

"I Just Want to Fit In"

Probably the most common thing we heard from LDS youth regarding peer pressure was their desire to fit in with friends at high school. This fitting in involves emotional acceptance from and social involvement with friends, which, in turn, promotes a sense of self-worth. School is a mini-society within which our children must interact with others their own age and with whom they must compete for acceptance.

The "coins of the realm" among adolescents generally are physical attractiveness and athletic ability. Youth with plain looks and limited sports skills have a more difficult time gaining acceptance among high school peers. Occasionally someone with an outgoing personality or an unusual artistic or musical ability will fit in. Others play the role of class clown to win attention, equating laughs with acceptance. Still others try to establish their identity or worth by engaging in risky or dangerous behavior such as drinking, fighting, or doing drugs.

Most of our kids are average, with average looks, average academic performance, average talent, and average athletic ability. Therefore, conformity to their friends' demands is what they have to offer in purchasing friendship. The desire to fit in is so strong that many LDS youth compromise their standards, hoping to facilitate their acceptance by their peers. Unfortunately, compromise often becomes the "coin of the realm" required to obtain social integration, popularity, and acceptance by the in crowd. Many youth would rather have leprosy than be ostracized, labeled as "weird," made fun of, or left out. Loneliness can be a powerful motivator. One young man stated his desire to be accepted by peers:

> My biggest pressure to not live the standards of the Church is definitely my friends. I don't know what it is, but I think it is a desire to fit in or be "popular." The problem is I'm a little bit shy, and so when I'm around friends I feel I have to make them like me, and sometimes I do things I know are wrong. But if I don't do these things, I am rejected and feel isolated.

A young woman confessed similar feelings:

> Pressures for me have been from wanting to fit in, from seeing my friends do things that aren't the best, and from not wanting to be made fun of. I think this makes it hard for me to fully understand what's right and wrong, and so sometimes I do things I regret later.

"Sometimes It's Hard to Know What's Right or Wrong"

A few years ago a television newsmagazine program reported on the replication of a famous psychological experiment about how peers influence perception. Solomon Asch, a Harvard psychologist, conducted the original study in the 1950s. He asked unsuspecting college students to match the length of a line drawn on a card to three other lines, drawn on another card. The match was obvious and could be correctly identified by virtually everyone 99 percent of the time. Peer pressure was introduced into the experiment by having trained students purposely select an incorrect line. Asch discovered that a group of seven or eight students produced the strongest peer pressure.

During the experiment, an unsuspecting student was seated at a table with seven trained students. One by one each of the trained student assistants, unbeknownst to the subject student, purposely selected the wrong line. The naive subject was placed next to last to allow six peers to choose an incorrect line first. Researchers discovered that one-third of the subjects immediately went along with the group and selected the same incorrect line. Others held out, but ultimately only a few went against the crowd and chose the correct answer every time.

Interestingly, the results of the recent study were much the same as a generation ago. The pressure to go along to get along is real with youth today. Later, when they were interviewed, some of the subjects said they were more afraid of "sticking out like a sore thumb" than being wrong. Others, however, may actually have had their perception altered by wanting to fit, coming to believe that the incorrect answer was correct. The *reality* of the peers became the *reality* of the subjects, even when that *reality* was not real at all.

This psychological phenomenon coincides with what several youth in our study stated:

Pressures against keeping the standards have come from wanting to fit in, seeing my friends do things that maybe are not the best, not wanting to be made fun of, and wanting to have friends. I think sometimes I don't fully understand what's right and wrong in situations when it's not obvious.

Sometimes I have let friends influence me. Because they would reject me, sometimes I have broken rules even though I know it is bad. It seems like it isn't important at the time. Afterward I feel bad about myself.

Our studies produced some results concerning peer influences that were particularly troubling. Two behaviors emerged for which LDS youth seem particularly susceptible to the influence of friends: cheating in school and premarital sex. Although LDS youth have considerably lower levels of delinquency, drug abuse, and premarital sex than their national peers, they cheat on school tests and assignments just as often as their non-LDS peers. Approximately seventy percent of both LDS and non-LDS high school students cheat on examinations or plagiarize written assignments or homework.

When asked why, LDS teens served up the old refrain, "Everyone does it." Some added that they were worried about admittance to a good college or university, that they wanted to qualify for a scholarship, or that they would be disadvantaged if they didn't join fellow students in cheating.

Regarding premarital sexual behavior, significantly fewer LDS youth than their national peers reported premarital sexual activity. Gospel teachings about chastity, therefore, do make a difference. The bad news, however, is that peer influences are overwhelmingly the driving force behind sexual immorality among LDS young people.[1] This was true for fifty LDS teenage girls who had become pregnant out of wedlock. What amazed us was that only one of the fifty girls had "actively" or "passionately" participated in the initiation of sexual behavior.

When asked why they had had sex the first time, half of the girls replied, "I don't know; it just happened." Further questioning revealed that their older boyfriends (usually two to four years older) pressured them to participate and that the girls lacked the courage to say, "Stop!" Other girls said they had initiated sex because they wanted to please their boyfriend or wanted him to like them.

Studies about the influence of peers may seem overwhelming, but we have repeatedly found that parents can *directly* influence the power peers have in the lives of their children. From our studies and experience we have discovered several specific and practical things parents can do minimize negative peer pressure and maximize positive peer influences.

Foster Good Friendships

We often feel helpless when it comes to influencing our children's choice of friends. To a certain degree, our children feel the same way. Often, they have little control over choosing who becomes their friend. In some cases they may lack the social skills to strike up friendships with young people that their parents would approve of, or they may be rebuffed by someone with whom they would like to associate. Indeed, much of the process of youth bonding *seems* to be largely determined by chance. But such is not the case. Parents can help their children to establish good friendships and benefit from positive influences.

Teach Friendship Skills

Parents often tell their children to make new friends, but they don't tell them how. "I sometimes would just take any friends that would make me part of their group," one young woman recalled. "I didn't know what else to do."

We parents often assume that our children know how to make friends. If we don't like the peer group they're hanging out with, we simply tell them to make new friends, as if they could do that with the snap of a finger. From the comments of many young people in our studies, we have learned that developing positive friendships is a skill that doesn't come as naturally to all of our children as we would like or may think. When parents understand this, they can be sensitive to the challenges facing their children. Being a true friend and cultivating good friendships is a skill that must be learned and practiced.

Family home evening may provide us with opportunities to teach friendship skills, including how to be good friends and how to get away from bad friends. Using the gospel of Jesus Christ as our foundation, we can also teach our families what it means to be a true friend. The leaders of the Church have given wise counsel concerning developing positive friendships. Their talks and teachings can serve as a basis for our parental teaching and counsel. Elder Malcolm S. Jeppsen taught that good friends are so valuable that they must be cultivated:

> Friendship is an extremely important part of your life. Someone has said *a true friend is someone who makes it easier to live the gospel of Jesus Christ.*
>
> Many of you young men [and young women] will be, at some time or another, approached by one of more of your "friends" who will entice you to do something you know you should not do—it might be something you know deep down inside will hurt your parents and your Father in Heaven. It may be violating the Word of Wisdom, for

example, or committing moral transgression, which is so displeasing to the Lord.

"No one will ever know," the so-called "friends" will tell you. "Besides, what difference will it make?"

My young friends, you don't have to reject your friends who are on the wrong path; you don't even have to give them up necessarily. You can be their caring friend, ready to help them when they are ready to be helped. You can talk to them and lift them and bear your testimony to them. Lead them by example.

But don't ever be led into displeasing your Father in Heaven by your friends who might ask that as a condition of being your friend, you must choose between their way and the Lord's way.

If that happens, choose the Lord's way and look for new friends. . . .

Choose your true friends wisely. They will provide the foundation of spiritual strength that will enable you to make difficult, extremely important decisions correctly when they come in your life.[2]

As children work their way through elementary school, junior high school, and high school, it is helpful for parents to teach them social skills that will help them make and keep friends. Children can be taught to be considerate of others, to be a friend to those less popular, and to be friendly and outgoing. Parents can also encourage their teenagers to be of service to others, helping with homework, offering rides home, making sure all youth are selected when sides are chosen for a game, offering encouragement in school activities, teaching a sports skill, or helping with chores.

One young man thanked his parents for teaching him friendship skills: "They taught me how to make friends with anyone, how to resolve issues with other people, how to discipline myself, be responsible for my choices, and respect others." Another young man complained when asked what his parents could have done to help him choose good friends: "It might have been helpful to have had lessons about how to make friends when I was young."

An adolescent who develops friendship skills will have more potential friends from whom to select *good* friends and will experience less rejection from peers.

Foster Friendships with Other Families

We should develop friendships with families that also have children. Doing so gives us an opportunity to model for our children skills involved in fostering friendships. Sharing wholesome activities with another family helps your children learn the give and take of true friendship. Visit an amusement park, go camping, have a picnic, attend a sporting event, or enjoy some other fun activity together. Invite children from the other family to join your family in a wide variety of activities. From such family-to-family interaction, friendships among teenagers may blossom. Even if close friendships do not emerge, the children will likely help each other in school and other settings. They may even speak up in each other's defense or give a positive character reference at a crucial time.

Participate in Wholesome Extracurricular Activities

Probably the most effective thing parents can do to help their children select good friends is to encourage them to participate in groups, organizations, and activities that will involve them with other good kids. In the *The Music Man*, Professor Harold Hill persuaded parents that any trouble in River City could be eliminated by a boys' band. In a similar vein, many youth credit their extracurricular activities with linking them with supportive friends. One young woman said:

> I usually made friends with people who were in similar activities as me, like track and cross-country. I was also in a few accelerated classes and got to know kids in them who were pretty good kids and were committed to school.

A young man explained how he used an extracurricular activity to exchange a rowdy bunch of friends for a more righteous group:

> If you've messed up and you need to start over with new friends, start a new extracurricular activity. You'll meet an entirely new group of people and have a fresh start. It may be a good idea to let your old friends know you're trying to

do better. If they don't want to change too, it won't be hard to say good-bye.

A young woman credited her parents for their support:

> My parents supported me in school and extracurricular activities that took up most of my time and kept me out of trouble. Also, I was with the best kids in these activities.

Although many extracurricular activities require fees, most parents recognize that the benefits greatly outweigh the costs. The time spent driving our children and their friends to and from various activities, coupled with the support they feel from our attendance at those activities, is a lucrative investment that yields emotional closeness in our families.

Positive extracurricular activities include athletic teams, band, drama, National Honor Society, choir, and clubs. Community activities—including local theater groups and service clubs—also offer opportunities for our children to associate with good youth. As a general rule, youth involved in these kinds of activities are serious about school and have less time, energy, or inclination to engage in delinquent behaviors.

Encourage Friendships with Members of the Church

The students we studied made it clear that most of their good friends were members of the Church and that most of their friends who sought to lead them astray were not members of the Church. Obviously, not all Church friends are good, and not all friends outside the Church are bad. But "Church friends" and participation in Church activities provide our children with additional sources of positive peer influences and spiritual support. As President Gordon B. Hinckley has taught:

> Look for your friends among members of the Church. Band together and strengthen one another. And when the time of temptation comes, you will have someone to lean on, someone to bless you and give you strength when you need it. That is what this Church is for, so that we can help one another in our times of weakness to stand on our feet, tall and straight and true and good.[3]

A large number of youth in our studies reported that they found their best friends at Church. "The friends I chose to spend my free time with were those I knew from seminary and Church classes," noted one young man. Another indicated that his parents encouraged him "to participate in seminary, Mutual activities, and other Church activities. These were the places where I found better friends."

For teens to participate in activities with their Church friends often requires considerable parental sacrifice as parents provide rides or give up the family car for a day or evening. In some cases, travel distances can be considerable, but parents in our

studies understood that nurturing valuable friendships is worth the time and expense.

Another way parents can facilitate LDS friendships is to host activities for LDS youth. One young
woman said:

> My parents were willing to help us gather
> LDS kids together. Although it meant opening
> their home to a bunch of noisy teenagers, it gave
> us a place to be together and build friendships.
> My parents made sure I was able to attend all
> Church events—even if it meant driving hours
> away to get to a youth dance. It meant we could
> build relationships with other LDS kids.

Many of our children's friends who are not members of the Church also have high ideals and strong
values and can be supportive of Church standards.
However, some young people in our surveys mentioned that as their non-LDS friends grew older, they
often drifted into activities inappropriate for members of the Church. This was a source of pain and
usually ended in estrangement. One young woman
reported:

> I grew up in California. Most of my friends
> were not LDS. My friends were great until our
> senior year. Then they all began partying and
> drinking. It was very hard not to join in. I just
> wouldn't go to the parties. This was the best way
> for me to keep away from the drinking and drugs.
> I eventually was not as close to these friends and

developed much closer relationships with kids at Church.

A young man told a similar story:

> At first all my friends were nonmembers and had high standards. But as we got older, they started drinking and smoking and doing other things that I would not participate in. I then decided to be with other people with standards like mine, members of the Church. This was difficult at first, but it is what I wanted to do. My old friends would still continue to bother me about going to their parties, but I just said, "No thanks."

A sizable majority of high school seniors today engage in behavior that should be shunned by members of the Church. More than 80 percent drink alcohol, nearly 75 percent engage in premarital sexual behavior, and about 35 percent experiment with illegal drugs.

In areas where few Church members live, LDS youth face the difficult decision of whether to date outside the Church. As noted above, many non-LDS teens have different values, especially regarding chastity. One young man said, "I wish my parents had not let me date people not of my faith!" A young woman also advised against such dating:

> Don't date nonmembers. Bottom line, it is just too hard—even the so-called "nice guys." Good can never be a relative term; members of the Church [should] realize the absolutes.

Nonmembers have different and twisted versions of what is right and wrong.

Dating outside the Church is a difficult issue that must be examined in the context of personal circumstances. Certain rules may not apply in every situation and to every person. Fortunately, we have the gift of the Holy Ghost to direct us in doing what is best for each of our children.

Welcome Friends into Your Home

Another good way for parents to help their teens develop friendships with good youth is to make their home available as a place to hang out. One young man said, "My parents always encouraged me to invite my friends over, which in turn encouraged me to have friends that I wasn't ashamed to have in our home." Another young man said:

> I can't praise my parents enough for just opening up our home to my friends. They always fed us and let us play Nintendo and bring girls over. My friends and I would rather be at my house on Friday night than out partying or driving around. This has kept us out of lots of trouble.

Parents can increase the attraction of their home by making friends feel welcome. This not only strengthens friendships among the youth but also creates ties between parents and their children's friends. "My parents made an effort to get to know my friends and to welcome them into our home" said one young man. Another added:

> My parents were very involved in my life. They were friends with my friends, so it was fun to bring friends to my home. My parents also taught me about being kind.

One young woman blamed her parents' lack of hospitability for some of the trials she faced as a teenager:

> I wish my parents had encouraged me to have more activities at our house. The trials I faced always happened at someone else's home. I don't think my friends would have even considered doing certain things in our home.

A young man reported:

> We weren't allowed to have friends over very often. I think our family could've benefited from more interaction with people. I don't think we were as welcoming as we should have been.

Teenagers make a lot of noise, empty a refrigerator with astonishing speed, and put extraordinary wear and tear on the furniture, but welcoming them into your home can protect your children against inappropriate peer pressure.

Minimize Negative Peer Pressure

Parents can do only so much to guide their children in choosing friends. Then comes the task of helping children resist the negative peer pressure they undoubtedly will encounter. In public school settings, LDS youth are thrown into contact with a wide variety of associates who invite and sometimes pressure them to do things against gospel standards. Many youth echoed the tension created by having to associate with young people with low moral values and standards.

One young man stated, "My friends' standards were not as high as mine, but they were the best choices in the school. I don't think my parents realize just how low most students' standards at high school were."

Normally youth must face such pressures without immediate parental support. But parents are not helpless in this struggle.

Take a Stand

When asked how they had resisted negative peer pressure while in high school, young adult college students overwhelmingly replied, "Make a clear statement of your values and then stick to them." One young woman explained it this way:

> I made sure all of my friends knew what I believed from day one. After that, if they asked me to do something against my beliefs I would just laugh. I would say, "You know I don't do that. Why are you even asking?"

A young man reported a similar experience:

> Be firm about what you believe. Never compromise because the first time you do you will lose the respect of your peers.

One young woman reported:

> My friends all knew my standards and didn't invite me to participate in activities they knew I'd be uncomfortable with. In fact, they would warn me against things (movies or song lyrics) that they knew I would not be comfortable seeing or hearing.

Another young woman reported the same experience:

> In Minnesota there are hardly any Mormons. Everyone knew who I was, and they knew my standards. It was to the point where they wouldn't let me do bad things, even if I had wanted to.

The implication of these and similar experiences is that parents should encourage their children to share their personal behavior standards with their friends during the initial stages of friendship. Latter-day Saint youth should look for an opportunity to say something like, "I am LDS, and as you probably know we don't drink or smoke." Two benefits result from youth sharing personal standards early on with their friends. First, they will probably experience considerably less pressure to violate gospel standards because many, although not all, of their friends will refrain from exerting overt pressure on them to do so. Second, some of their friends will become supporters who will buffer them from negative pressure by others.

Avoiding Bad Situations

The young adults we surveyed acknowledged that while in high school they knew what went on at parties and other after-school events. Many of them reported that avoiding situations where they would be pressured to smoke, drink, do drugs, and have premarital sex was the best way to resist pressure from friends to participate in such activities. A young woman stated:

> Mostly I just never placed myself anywhere there could be a problem with keeping my standards. If I ever found myself trapped, I just walked away without any lengthy discussion.

Many young adults credited their parents for helping them avoid bad situations. One young man said:

> Sometimes my parents wouldn't allow me to go to certain activities because they knew the situations would bring me down. They made sure I knew that it wasn't because they didn't trust me. They just knew it was a place where the Spirit couldn't be.

Using Parents as an Excuse

Despite their best efforts, youth occasionally find themselves in situations rife with temptation. Several young adults appreciated that their parents gave them the right to invoke parental disapproval and potential punishment as an excuse for refusing to do something against gospel standards.

"My father said if I was ever in a bad situation, I could use him as an excuse to get out of it," one young man confided. A young woman stated that she had her parents' permission, if the need arose to tell friends, "My parents would kill me if I did that. I would be grounded forever." This approach allowed many youth to resist temptation without losing face with friends.

Research has repeatedly demonstrated that peer influence is the most powerful force a teenager faces when deciding whether to become involved in drinking, smoking, drugs, premarital sex, and other immoral behaviors. LDS youth experience considerable pressure from their friends in school to violate the Word of Wisdom and the law of chastity. Fortunately, we can assist our children in choosing good friends, and we can fortify them in their struggles to live righteously in the face of negative peer pressure.

Notes

1. For a detailed report and results of this study, see Brent L. Top and Bruce A. Chadwick, "Protecting Purity," *BYU Magazine*, vol. 57, no. 3 (Summer 2003), 46–54.

2. Malcolm S. Jeppsen, "Who Is a True Friend?" *Ensign*, May 1990, 45; emphasis added.

3. Gordon B. Hinckley, *Teachings of Gordon B. Hinckley* (Salt Lake City: Deseret Book, 1997), 429.

Chapter 5

Establish Firm but Fair Boundaries

Many years ago, Elder Boyd K. Packer recounted a story from his youth that has an important application to parents. He told of a valuable lesson he learned when he, as a ten-year-old, had the responsibility of overseeing the irrigation of the family orchard. Although the irrigation ditches had been cleared of debris in the spring, by midsummer they were once again choked with all kinds of weeds. The "turn" for irrigation water from the canal came infrequently, so every drop of water was valuable and needed to get to the trees.

> One day, in charge of the irrigation turn, I found myself in trouble. As the water moved down the rows choked with weeds, it would flood in every direction. I raced through the puddles trying to build up the bank. As soon as I

had one break patched up, there would be another.

A neighbor came through the orchard. He watched for a moment, and then with a few vigorous strokes of the shovel he cleared the ditch bottom [of weeds] and allowed the water to course through the channel he had made.

"If you want the water to stay in its course, you'll have to make a place for it to go," he said.[1]

In a way, our children are like the irrigation water. To do what they are supposed do and become what they are supposed to become, they need to be channeled in the right direction. That is where we as parents can help. Teaching principles and values and establishing family rules based on those values help our children stay on course and fulfill their higher destiny. Without the guidance afforded by family rules, their lives become like irrigation water in a weed-choked ditch—flooding over its banks, flowing in any and all directions, failing to accomplish a desired end.

The high school students in our studies vividly described the weed-choked world through which our children must navigate—the unrelenting pressure to drink, smoke, engage in premarital sex, do drugs, cheat on schoolwork, skip class, and fall prey to other temptations. Unfortunately, this has become a characteristic of modern high school culture. Most of their classmates drink, most are involved with pornography, many are promiscuous, and a substantial number do drugs. These kinds of "weeds" that fill the "ditches" of life have the potential to do even greater damage to our youth than the damage done to fruit trees when they fail to get irrigated. If we want to assist our young people to avoid spiritually and physically destructive evils, we must provide them with proper direction.

Parents oversee the establishment of family rules to help their children navigate the moral minefields of school, community, and society. Principle-based rules help clear the ditches and provide a proper channel that will help children stay on course and away from situations fraught with temptation and danger. Considerable research over the years has demonstrated that young people who grow up in homes without rules or guiding principles and who are not held accountable fail to learn to control their behavior. Resulting hedonism, the constant pursuit of pleasure and excitement, results in self-destructive behavior. Lacking self-control, such youth often act impulsively and do things they later regret. In addition, they are overly susceptible to influence from friends.

Parents must not only ensure the establishment of rules in the home but must also monitor the behavior of their children. When youth disobey or defy family rules, parents must do one of the most difficult and least desirable of all parental duties— they must provide discipline. These three parental responsibilities—establish family rules, monitor behavior, and administer appropriate discipline—constitute parental regulation that is imperative in the lives of young people.

It is of no use to set rules and then not determine whether your children are obeying them. Also, it does little good to monitor behavior if there are no meaningful consequences for disobedience. Of course, discipline without rules is capricious and unfair, and our children, whatever their age, will quickly recognize it as such. Because of the importance of these principles, the next three chapters deal with setting rules, monitoring compliance, and administering discipline.

Successful regulation of behavior contributes to a more loving, peaceful family life and to the development of self-mastery in young adults. It also helps maintain an environment in which Mom and Dad's influence can be more powerful and their instruction in principles of righteousness more effective.

The Blessings of Boundaries

The eminent French sociologist Emile Durkheim observed that when war, depressions, or economic booms cause the laws or rules in a society to rapidly change, such societies have higher rates of suicide than do more stable societies. He demonstrated through pioneering statistical analysis how a lack of rules, which he called "anomy," could create such severe anxiety in some people that they opt for suicide rather than to continue to live with social uncertainty.

The adolescent years can be a particularly stressful time for our children—a time fraught with confusion as they exert their independence, question rules of childhood, and develop rules of adulthood. Some youth are not sure which childhood rules still apply and which adulthood rules should begin to apply.

Parents, teachers, and Church leaders can help reduce this emotionally painful confusion by establishing permanent rules of conduct long before children move through the turbulent teenage years. Youth need to be given a firm foundation upon which they can build—a clear and lasting view of right and wrong that can lead them like a beacon.

Parents play a major role in this process by establishing family rules, which are modified as their children age and mature. Some parents *mistakenly* believe that giving their teenagers unlimited freedom makes them happy and fosters their independence. In reality, such parents may be creating confusion in their children about what is right and what is wrong. This in turn may lead to youthful mistakes that have serious consequences.

We were surprised that more young people in our studies complained about too few family rules than complained about too many restrictions. One young man observed, "My parents did not set rules or guidelines. I never knew or understood what standards should guide me until it was too late." A young woman voiced the same opinion: "They should have been more strict and consistent in their rules and punishments." Another youth stated, "I wish they had not been so relaxed with me. I was able to learn from my mistakes, which were many, but it would have been nice to have had a few more restrictions."

Some teens blamed a lack of family rules for their falling into sin. One young man said:

> One thing they [my parents] did wrong was to give me too much freedom when I was not really ready to handle it. As a result, it led to some poor judgment calls that brought about some unnecessary trials.

Another young man also desired greater structure in the home:

> I wish they had been more strict and more disciplinarian toward me and my brother, especially toward my brother. He now suffers from drug addiction because they did not try to control him away from drugs. He lacks an understanding of how to be a man.

Although a few young people enjoyed being liberated from family rules, most felt that a lack of rules was a sign that their parents did not care about them or about what happened to them. "I wish they had set more rules," one young woman said. "I know that it is weird to say, but their lack of rules made me feel they did not care." One young man said:

> They set a curfew and wanted to know where I was going and whom I'd be with. This showed me that they cared about me and wanted me to be safe. The friends whose parents let them have "freedom"—no curfew or checking in—are the ones who got in trouble.

It is not surprising that young adults often look back on family rules with a far different perspective than when they were younger and living at home. An LDS college student said:

> At the time, I thought my parents were trying to control a lot of my life with curfews, making me go to Church, not allowing me to participate in activities on Sunday, and so on. But I see now how that actually helped me have more options and freedom in my future.

A young woman added:

> I hated having a curfew! None of my friends had curfews, and we were all good kids. So I couldn't understand why I needed to have one. My parents were adamant about me having one because the prophet told us to. It wasn't until I left home that I realized what a blessing it truly was, and I'm grateful they did not give in to my nagging.

A number of young people complained that their

parents micromanaged them by creating too many strict family rules. "There were too many nitpicky rules. They were too strict on curfew at prom times," one young woman said. A young man echoed this sentiment:

> Our house had a thousand rules. I will just use one example to illustrate what home life was like. At dinnertime the main focus was more about good manners and why we didn't do our chores, rather than on "How was your day?" or "How was baseball practice?"

Parents need to steer a course between the two extremes. It is important to avoid overcontrolling on one hand and leaving youth totally on their own on the other hand. Our children, particularly our teens, need and actually desire (although they may never admit it and even fight against it) the structure provided by family rules. They welcome guidance in expanding their growing independence and freedom. You may not often see that positive and welcoming attitude in their countenances, but it is there nonetheless.

The number and formality of family rules can vary from two or three guiding principles to a detailed, multi-page family constitution. The format is not as important as building family, Church, school, community, and societal expectations into the rules. Our children understand the Word of Wisdom and usually don't need a detailed list of rules to follow it. On the other hand, the guiding principle of "Be good" is probably a little too general for an average child. Principle-based rules somewhere in between work best.

One family used the guidelines contained in the *For the Strength of Youth* pamphlet. "My parents taught me every rule in the *For the Strength of Youth* pamphlet, and they made me follow the rules to a tee," one teen said. "Through this, my parents taught me the importance of following the prophet."

Rules are generally designed to keep young people away from situations where they will likely be exposed to temptation. Thus, parents establish curfews to limit teens' participation in late-night or all-night activities, which often involve drinking, drugs, immorality, and other delinquent activities. In the past, parents often imposed rules to prevent steady dating. This type of rule often loses its effectiveness in today's hanging-out-with-friends culture.

Our studies have confirmed that immorality occasionally occurs between young men and women who are barely acquainted. They may "hook up" while hanging out in a large group setting and then engage in immoral activities. As a result of the worldliness our children encounter today, we need to establish curfews, rules regarding the kinds of friends our children may associate with, and whether adult chaperons will be required at certain activities.

Family rules are a work in progress and need to change as children mature and demonstrate an ability to manage their lives. Guidelines should shift from specific rules to general principles as young people demonstrate their maturity through righteous and responsible actions and attitudes.

In our studies, we have observed some things that can help parents regulate their families and bless their children with proper boundaries. How well they work in your family will depend on the effort you exert.

Allow Children Input

It comes as no surprise that teenagers want a say in the rules that govern their lives. A few teens will argue for near total freedom from constraint, but most are willing to work with their parents in setting family rules that will bring peace to the home and protect them from dangers in their social world. Young people appreciate the chance to help make rules, and parents may be surprised at how reasonable teens can be in crafting guidelines. A young woman described how this process worked in her family:

> My parents let us make our own rules. For example, we chose a curfew and a punishment for breaking it. We as a family, but mostly the daughters, picked a curfew of 10:30 p.m. on week-nights, 1 a.m. on Friday nights, and midnight on

Saturday nights. If we were even one minute late we got punished. The established punishment was for every minute we were late, we lost one hour from our next date. It was what we chose.

Several young people in our studies noted that they had to exert themselves to have even minimal influence in setting family rules. "We had a family constitution that dictated all of our rules," one young man said, adding, "I had to fight for any input!" A young woman shared a similar account:

> It isn't often that we, the children, are decision makers in family matters or have a say or vote about family rules. I wish my parents wouldn't always take the "I'm the parent, you're the kid" attitude.

Youth who don't have the opportunity to seriously discuss with their parents the nature of family rules are much more likely to rebel and feel that their parents overcontrol them. When teens have some say in family rules and associated discipline, it becomes more difficult for them to fight against the rules or resent the consequences. As one young man observed, "It is pretty hard for me to rebel against my parents since I helped make the rules for the family!"

Make Rules Clear

Family rules or expectations must be clear if young people are to comply with them. One young man voiced this concern:

Their discipline [rules] at times was inconsistent, and this made it very difficult to predict what they wanted. It has caused me to be flighty at times with people I can't figure out. It has also caused me to hesitate in certain situations where I feel semi-threatened.

A young woman echoed this confusion:

My parents neglected to clearly define family rules, values, and beliefs. Also, they neglected to maintain family traditions. In other words, they neglected to provide understandable boundaries for us.

Another young woman voiced this resentment:

I did not like the fact that they did not explain why the rules were the way they were. Their answer was always just "Because." I wish that they had explained why and what would happen if I chose not to follow. I also wish they had realized that just because a rule worked for one child doesn't mean it will work for all the others.

It is difficult for young men and young women to feel good about rules they don't understand or that appear to be arbitrary rather than linked to an important and understandable principle. One young man explained that in his family, "The family standards were always well understood. I knew how much freedom I had and that it would last as long as I made good choices and kept the rules."

Because our rules may not be as clear as we

parents believe, it is important that we discuss them often, giving our children an opportunity to raise issues and express their feelings about rules and the reasons behind them. This is fostered by an environment of open communication where our children can feel "invested" in the process of family regulation rather than feel like lowly subjects before a totalitarian dictator.

One young man had meaningful discussions with his parents when he came in at night. "I enjoyed late-night talks with my parents, usually after coming in late. They explained the rules and why things are the way they are." Rousing themselves from sleep, these good parents would try to explain their hopes for him and how coming home on time related to those dreams. Similarly, a young woman gave a detailed description of how she and her parents discussed family rules and sometimes adjusted them for a given occasion:

> It was clear in our home that if we wanted to enjoy freedom, there was a set family guidelines we needed to operate within. The old saying "Our house, our rules" applied to my parents. But they were very understanding and did not have overly restrictive rules. For example, I did not have a curfew in high school. Instead of a set curfew, we would take each activity and analyze it. Then both my parents and I would come up with a reasonable time for me to return home. We would discuss the activity and why I needed to be at a

place for a certain amount of time. The decision would be made, and I was satisfied.

They would not let me hang out with friends late on a school night. But they were reasonable. If I wanted to go to a party, I would tell my parents where the party was and who I thought would be there, and that I wanted to come home at 2 a.m. After agreeing to a time, I couldn't be late. In essence, I made the curfew and needed to live up to it. They would let me go to the party, knowing I would not smoke, drink, or take drugs. They trusted me to behave. I really appreciated how they worked with me, yet I realize it probably would not work with all kids.

This approach sounds like a great deal of work, but it taught this young woman to think for herself, to seek the Spirit for help in applying rules and principles to her life, and to be more independent. Discussion helps our children understand the *whys* of family rules. Achieving understanding through discussion and loving guidance is integral to helping them mature. In addition, these occasions give us a golden opportunity to glimpse into the activities and feelings of our children.

Focus on Important Issues

The old admonition "Don't sweat the small stuff" applies to family rules. What is large stuff and small stuff will vary from family to family and even from child to child. Parents, with input from children, need to identify what values and related behaviors are important to their family and then craft suitable rules or principles. Most parents will want to set principle-based rules that foster spirituality in their children.

Thus, participation in family home evening, family prayer, and family scripture study is spelled out in the rules of many families. Church attendance, priesthood and scouting advancement, Young Women awards, and Church service are also on the "large stuff" list for many families. Together, parents and children decide which rules or practices will work to make the gospel a living force in their family and in their personal lives.

Friends, leisure pursuits, extracurricular activities, dating, and other social activities are also generally considered important to both parents and children, although maybe for different reasons. Because of the importance of education, rules related to homework, attendance, classes, grades, extra-curricular activities, and respect for teachers usually emerge in most families. Many young people are convinced that their parents' academic expectations for them are too high—maybe even unrealistic. But most are willing to work hard and sincerely try. Rules should focus on effort, improvement, and perseverance, rather than merely on grades or test scores.

Finally, according to the youth in our surveys,

most families have rules pertaining to family chores. It may not seem like a big thing to assign certain tasks to each child, but it is vital for more reasons than just keeping the house clean. Giving chores to teenagers is an essential facet of parental regulation. As we will see in the next section, having rules about household chores and family responsibilities is directly linked to the overall character development of our children.

Assign Family Chores

Assigning family members age-appropriate chores and household responsibilities is, in a way, a laboratory experience in the "family school," where parents teach real lessons about responsibility and accountability. Because these lessons are so important, we should begin teaching them while our children are young. Assigned chores can begin as simple tasks that even a toddler can do. As the children get older the tasks can become more complex and demanding.

Completing tasks around the home helps our children—whatever their ages—develop a sense of responsibility and recognize how family members depend on each other and how their individual behavior has consequences for the whole family. If a meal is delayed because of insufficient clean dishes, the child responsible for doing the dishes learns a valuable lesson from the grumbling of those who have to wait to eat. One young adult woman remembered how her parents assigned different dinnertime chores to each child so that the children would not only work together as a team but also recognize that family members depended on each other:

> Each of us children had a dinnertime job. It rotated each week. One would set the table, another would clear off the table, another would load the dishwasher, and another would put away the clean dishes. One job had to be done before the next one could be done, and so on. If one kid didn't do his job it affected all of us and "backed up" everything and delayed dinner. One rule in particular motivated us. Before we could have our dessert, the dishes had to be cleared off the table. So whoever had that job was greatly encouraged (sometimes not so pleasantly) by the rest of the family to make sure it got done.
>
> I can see now that it wasn't just about dessert or clean dishes. Mom and Dad were using these chores and the rules associated with them to help us to learn by experience about consequences and how all of us are dependent upon one another.

Once chores are assigned, parents need to ensure that family members complete their assigned tasks. This parental regulation will have immediate effects on daily family life as well as yield long-term dividends in character development. Elder L. Tom Perry declared:

Children need to be taught the joy of honest labor and experience the satisfaction which results from seeing a job well done. . . . I am shocked as I become aware that in so many homes, many of the children do not know how to make a bed, care for their clothing, squeeze a tube of toothpaste to conserve, turn off the lights, set a proper table, mow a lawn, or care for a vegetable garden. These simple acts of cleanliness, order, and conservation will bless their lives every day they live and prepare them to become self-sufficient when they reach an age when they must be out on their own.[2]

One young man echoed this idea:

My parents established rules and consequences that forced me to be responsible and honest. My parents always made me do chores. I hated them at the time, but they made me responsible. I also acquired many skills and talents from cleaning, cooking, etc., which I so very much appreciate now!

A young woman, looking back, expressed a similar feeling:

I wish my parents had been more strict in seeing that I did my household chores—teaching me how to clean, cook, and take care of myself.

A young man also bemoaned the fact that his parents had not "forced" him to learn basic survival skills:

I wish they had not spoiled me so much and taught me how to work, like how to cook, fix a car, and so on.

Numerous studies have found that family chores can be a great opportunity for family members to work together, foster feelings of closeness, and learn the value of work. This is particularly important in this day and age when our society has moved away from an agrarian society in which daily chores were a matter of survival.

A father recounted how as a youth his family lived on a small farm. They had two cows, a coop full of chicks, and a large garden, for which the water turn always came in the middle of the night. While growing up, this father helped his own father feed the animals, gather the eggs, milk the cows, and plant, weed, and harvest the large family garden.

In his teenage years the family moved to a larger home in a city subdivision. The son was elated that his chores would shrink to mowing the lawn once a week in the summer and shoveling the snow from the sidewalk in the winter. Much to his surprise and disappointment, his father sat him down and explained that because they no longer lived on the farm and had "outside chores," they would now have "inside chores"—helping keep the house clean and organized. This teenage boy and his father joined his mother and sisters in washing dishes three nights each week and cleaning two rooms each Saturday.

At first, the young man thought it unfair "for a man to do women's work." His father's example, however, taught him how wrong his thinking had been. From those "inside chores" this teenage boy learned valuable lessons of responsibility, dependability, and service that served him throughout his life—particularly as a husband and father. Today his grateful wife appreciates his wise father for teaching him the need for a man to do what was once considered women's work.

Every wife and mother appreciates the helping hand of her husband in keeping the house clean and caring for the children. Likewise, employers and coworkers appreciate someone who has learned to accept less-desirable, low-profile assignments and who does more than just his share for the common good. Important lessons learned at home by doing chores will bless our family now and our children's families in years to come.

The shared experience of completing tasks together often generates feelings of attachment among family members. Time spent together working also provides parents with another opportunity to talk to children, listen to them, and teach them life lessons more effectively than through lecturing. Likewise, practical experience with chores will help children develop a strong work ethic as well as homemaking skills.

Attach Fair and Reasonable Consequences

Young people are quick to notice hypocrisy and injustice, especially when they perceive themselves as the victims of both. Children should be allowed some degree of input in both establishing family rules and in negotiating the consequences for disobedience to those rules. As noted earlier, youth who help frame family rules and associated consequences accept, defend, and uphold the penalties. Occasionally it may be necessary for parents to give more costly consequences than their teens deem appropriate. But there will also be occasions when parents need to reign in their teens' enthusiasm in assigning consequences to breaking family rules.

Justice seems to demand that all children in a family be treated equally, and the youth in our studies voiced support for equality before the law. A young man stated:

> I really appreciated that my mom and dad treated all us kids alike. They were very fair in sharing love and attention. Also, the rules applied to everyone in the family.

On the other hand, several youth complained that their parents did not treat all of the children the same. A young man exclaimed, "My younger brothers and sisters got away with murder!" A young woman concurred, "I wish they had applied the rules the same to all the kids. It seemed like they got more lenient with the younger kids."

Although equal treatment is best, there may be occasions when rules should be adapted to fit ages and circumstances. One family had an Indian Placement Program student live in their home for several years who posed unique challenges. The father explained:

> Our Navajo son didn't do as well in school as our biological sons were expected to do. When he wasn't grounded for getting a C- in one of his classes, one of our sons demanded to know why. "If I get a C, I get in big trouble. Why doesn't he?" When I explained to him that because of the unique challenges his "Navajo brother" had faced in life, it wouldn't be fair to hold him to the same set of academic expectations and rules that we had for the rest of the family. I explained that it was necessary to cut a little slack sometimes because "where much is given much is required." When my sons understood this they stopped complaining about what they had perceived as unfairness.

A few young people applauded their parents for differentiating between the children and adjusting how they applied rules to each of them. A young adult college student stated:

> One thing I love about how my parents raised my siblings and me is that they did not deal with each of us or discipline each of us exactly the

same. Rather, they did precisely what we needed. Sometimes we didn't think it was fair, but because they loved each of us and viewed us as individuals, they treated us the way each of us needed.

As a general rule parents should try to treat their children equally. Give each child a fair share of time, attention, and family resources, and hold each accountable for keeping family rules. But challenge the gifted child, and go easy on the slow child. This is one of those judgment calls for which parents receive such a large salary! Fortunately, we have the promise that the Holy Ghost will guide us in making critical judgments and adjustments.

Adjust Rules As Children Mature

Most parents recognize the maturation of their teens and grant them greater freedoms and privileges, as well as responsibilities. A senior in high school will most likely have a later curfew than a sixth-grader. A fourteen-year-old may be expected to do more around the house than a four-year-old. As teens demonstrate their ability to abide by family rules and govern themselves, they earn greater trust. Greater trust should translate into greater freedom. Our children understand this and expect us to understand and practice it too.

When we don't adjust the rules as children emotionally and spiritually mature, as evidenced by their actions and attitudes, they may feel that nothing they do will ever be good enough to warrant greater trust and freedom. The old notion of self-fulfilling prophecy then comes into play. Continually treating them like immature children will cause them to act like immature children.

One young man voiced this complaint: "My parents did not adapt the rules for me as I got older, and conflict resulted." One young woman couldn't figure out why the rules became tougher as she grew older, especially since she felt she had earned her parents' trust. "I did not like that they made the curfew and permission to go places more restrictive when I turned 18."

One young woman was especially upset that her parents did not recognize her status as a college student:

> A major source of contention between my parents and me was a curfew. It was one thing to have a strict curfew in high school, but after moving away to college and coming home to visit for the summers and having them tell me to be home before 11:30 or midnight was ridiculous. My parents should have adapted the rules after I became an adult.

Moving out of the home emancipates young adults, so rules for them need to be renegotiated. A curfew is fine for a returning college student, but the student and parents need to discuss the appropriate time. Too often we discourage our youth by giving them greater responsibilities as they get older without granting them greater freedom and trust. All children, particularly teenagers, need rules and guidelines to give structure and direction to their lives as they make the transition from childhood to adulthood.

If parents have an open mind, most teens will readily agree to a reasonable set of family rules. Young people will even accept some variation in rules and application to siblings if they are reasonable and clearly explained. Keeping the parent-child dialogue going will assist in making suitable adjustments to family rules.

Throughout the scriptures we see the mercy and goodness of God in giving his children commandments—not to stifle growth or fulfillment but to promote them. What a blessing it is to have commandments from a loving Father. When we begin to see the commandments and his expectations for us in the proper light, it becomes easier to live by his rules. That doesn't mean we won't make mistakes, but in general we want to be righteous when we see how the commandments protect, empower, and liberate us.

This same principle works for our children. Family rules, like the commandments, are not designed to make our children miserable. Rules, like commandments, provide clear direction for our children's lives.

Establishing family rules as part of our parental responsibility to discipline is, President Spencer W. Kimball taught, "one of the most important elements in which a mother and father can lead and guide and direct their children." It is more than a parental duty; it is an expression of parental love. "Setting limits to what a child can do means to that child that you love him and respect him," President Kimball added. "If you permit the child to do all the things he would like to do without any limits, that means to him that you do not care much about him."[3]

Just as Heavenly Father shows his love for us by giving us commandments that will enable us to become like him, we have an obligation to "clean out the ditches" and "dig a channel," so to speak, so that our children can become what they, we, and our Heavenly Father desire them to become. They are his children too. We are in partnership with him.

Establishing firm but fair boundaries protects children in the "weed-choked" world and liberates and empowers them to fulfill their foreordained missions in mortality.

Notes

1. Boyd K. Packer, "Inspiring Music—Worthy Thoughts," *Ensign*, November 1973, 27; see also Boyd K. Packer, *Memorable Stories and Parables by Boyd K. Packer* (Salt Lake City: Bookcraft, 1997), 78–89.

2. L. Tom Perry, "'Train Up a Child,'" *Ensign,* November 1988, 74.

3. Spencer W. Kimball, *The Teachings of Spencer W. Kimball,* ed. Edward L. Kimball (Salt Lake City, Bookcraft, 1982), 340–41.

Chapter 6

Keep Your Eyes Wide Open

Once the soil is prepared and the precious seeds are carefully planted, the wise gardener knows that his work is not completed but rather just beginning. He must be vigilant on many fronts. He must closely and carefully observe the garden to protect the tender plants against destructive insects. He must monitor the levels of moisture and sunlight his garden receives and be quick to note signs of inadequate fertilizer. Only in this way can he ensure that his garden produces a bounteous harvest of flowers, fruits, or vegetables. So it is with parenting.

Once family rules, principles, and guidelines are established, parents face the task of determining whether their children are moving toward adulthood in accordance with those rules, principles, and guidelines. In the disciplines of social science and child development, observing and evaluating that progress is often referred to as monitoring. Although difficult at times, and certainly time and energy consuming, monitoring is a crucial, even imperative, responsibility of parents.

A wise mother, one of the grandmothers in our study of experienced parents, noted that monitoring is a tough task:

> Following through on rules and chores is the toughest job as a parent. This is what makes parenting a full-time job. It takes time to check up and follow through on job assignments, music lessons, and doing what is right.

Keeping an eye on our children is absolutely essential in helping them develop the self-control that characterizes responsible adulthood. If a family has a fine set of rules, but the parents do not actively—consistently and conscientiously—monitor the behavior and activities of their children, particularly their teenagers, the rules are meaningless! For rules to be effective in guiding young people away from temptation, they must be enforced. That means parents have to keep their eyes wide open.

Effective monitoring, however, does not mean that we must spy on or interrogate our children. None of us would want to be treated that way. When monitoring goes beyond the boundaries of common decency, love, respect, and trust, nothing good results. Behavior may be modified temporarily by invasive monitoring tactics, but relationships inevitably suffer, and parents end up losing whatever influence they might have had in the lives of their children. Such was the case with a daughter who became incensed by her mother's unauthorized reading of her diary:

> My mom once read my journal without my permission. I really hated this! Because of this I never could trust my mom, and I wouldn't share anything of my life with her.

There are times, however, when parents do need to be intrusive. If there is a good chance a child is involved in self-destructive behavior, such as drug abuse, or in activities that could pose a serious threat to others, parents have an obligation to use whatever means, short of abuse or breaking the law, to find out what is going on. Extreme circumstances may warrant extreme measures.

Generally speaking, the most effective monitoring occurs when parents are interested and involved in their children's lives. This "normal" monitoring can provide parents with a great deal of information concerning how their children are doing and whether they're conforming to family rules. Spending time—quantity and quality time—with your children is an important way to monitor how things are going in their lives.

Monitoring requires that we be hands-on parents.

Our research shows that effective parental monitoring is linked to lower levels of sexual immorality and other forms of delinquency in children. The Partnership for a Drug-Free America reports that teens reared by involved and aware, but not overbearing, parents are less involved in illegal drug and alcohol abuse. According to the Partnership, being a hands-on parent requires that you do at least ten of the following:

- Monitor what your children watch on TV.
- Monitor your children's use of the Internet.
- Put restrictions on CDs, computer games, and videos your children buy.
- Know where your children are after school and on weekends.
- Make sure you are told the truth about your teenager's whereabouts.
- Know your teenager's academic performance.
- Impose a curfew.
- Make it clear that you would be "extremely upset" if your teen used marijuana or other drugs.
- Eat dinner with your children six or seven nights a week.
- Turn off the TV during dinner.
- Assign regular chores.
- Have an adult present when a teen comes home from school.[1]

We embrace these suggestions and, as Latter-day

Saints, we could probably add a few more suggestions that would be unique to our religious culture. Keeping our eyes wide open to what is happening in our children's lives also opens the door to recognition and praise of their efforts and accomplishments. Without keeping our eyes wide open, we may miss these golden opportunities. Likewise, keeping our eyes open lets us know how well our children understand and implement our teachings. Without monitoring, we will never know how and when to adjust our teachings and family rules or when to administer discipline.

Effective monitoring requires three things: asking the right questions, talking to the right people, and watching for warning signs.

Ask the Right Questions

The best source of information about our children is our children themselves. Open and ongoing family communication will provide parents with vital information about how their sons and daughters are behaving and what they are thinking and feeling about important things. Real communication, however, requires more than one-word, single-syllable, unrecognizable grunts in answer to our questions.

As an invitation to converse, a parent may ask, "How was your day?" To which the teen may respond, "Fine." An inquiry into the teen's school day may be met with such deep and descriptive comments as, "Okay." To which a parent may have nothing more profound to add than merely, "Good." That isn't communication. Such a "conversation" neither helps teens to know of our love and interest nor helps us to know what is really going on in their lives.

Starting when our children our young, we need to nurture discussions with them and cultivate them as important sources of information, despite their occasional reluctance. We do this by asking questions that can't be answered with one word. Asking the right questions and expecting our children to provide appropriate answers is vital to effective monitoring.

One young woman in our study praised her parents' question-asking abilities:

> They always paid attention to what was going on at school, what grades I was getting, classes I was taking, and so on. They always asked whom I was going with and what I was doing. The main thing was they had a constant interest in me.

If we begin talking to our children while they are young about what is going on in their lives, they will not, as teens, feel that we are spying on them merely by asking questions. They will have become accustomed to the questioning.

Over the past several years, the Partnership for a Drug-Free America has conducted an effective advertising campaign directed at parents. One of the primary messages of these clever public-service ads has been to tell parents to ask certain important questions:

- Who are you going with?
- What are you going to be doing?
- Where will you be?
- When will you be home?

One ad shows a teenage boy with spiked purple hair and rings in his pierced ears and eyebrows listening to heavy metal music. As he leaves the house, he says to his mother, "I'll be back by eleven." His mother then asks, "Who are you going to be with?" As her questions fade away, a voice declares, "Let your children be who they are, but know where they are going and what they are doing."

Another ad shows several teens speaking to their mothers and fathers and saying things such as, "You were the worst parent. You made my life miserable by insisting on knowing where I was going and who I was with! You were always butting in by wanting to know what was going in my life. You embarrassed me by making me call when I was going to be late." The ad ends with each of the teens saying, "Thanks."

The message is clear. Even when our children may roll their eyes or express displeasure with our questions and monitoring, they appreciate it—both now and later. We need to understand that monitoring is essential even if we don't hear their gratitude until much later.

Our studies of LDS families over the past decade confirmed that those parents who utilize the who, what, where, and when questions are the most effective at parental monitoring. In fact, the youth themselves have confirmed that asking the right questions is often even more important than rules. One young woman said:

> We never really had strict laid-down family rules, but my parents knew what I was doing, especially my mom. She knew how I was spending my allowance. My parents knew my friends because they usually came to my house to meet me. We did not have many rules, but I had to make sure that my parents knew what I was doing.

Another teen said:

> My parents allow me quite a lot of freedom, but they absolutely insist on knowing where I am going and who I am with.

A second young man credited his parents' diligence in keeping track of him with helping him avoid problems:

> My parents always had to know where I was going, with whom, for how long, etc. Also, Mom was always waiting up for me when I got home. I think this kept me honest and out of trouble.

A young woman described a similar relationship with her parents:

> They were always asking me questions about my life. They always asked me, "Where are you going?" "Who are you going with?" and "How long will you be gone?" They always encouraged me to be involved in things and with others outside our home; they just wanted to know all the details. Their interest really helped me be the kind of person I wanted to be.

Keeping their eyes open through talking and listening to children, particularly teens, allows parents to regularly offer needed support and make necessary path corrections.

Surprisingly, several youth complained that their parents did not ask enough questions about their comings and goings. A young man complained:

> My parents did not pry enough into my life. They would not give their opinion about things that I wanted to do. They didn't seem to care.

Another bemoaned that his parents knew little about what was going on in his life:

> My parents really weren't very aware of my life. When I turned 16 my father basically stayed out of my life. I had no curfew as long as I called when I was going to be really late. I was never punished. They just left me to live my own life. For some reason, they just weren't interested in me.

A young woman stated:

> I wish my parents would ask more questions about my life, get to know my friends, my activities, and my challenges.

When parents fail to show interest in their children and their activities, children feel that their parents don't really care about them or about what happens to them. A reasonable level of questioning will assure your children that you love them and sincerely care about them.

On the other hand, a few youth complained that their parents were too invasive in keeping track of where they were going and what they were doing. A young man said:

> If I was late or forgot to tell them where I was going, they would track me down for sure—whether it be by calling my friends' houses or showing up there! It was embarrassing, and I felt it was a little overprotective.

A young woman hated the third degree her parents gave the boys who came calling:

> The cross-examination of my guy friends was always traumatic for me. I wish my parents had trusted me more to choose good boyfriends.

Many young people in our studies said that heavy-handed attempts to pry into their lives would most likely generate resistance and perhaps encourage outright lying. A young man described how he resisted his parents' attempts to learn what he was doing because he felt they were guilty of heavy-handed prying:

> I told them as little as possible. They would try to gain information by asking questions, but I would usually answer vaguely.

He admitted, however, that shutting out his parents created negative consequences:

> I often reacted against my parents in high school and would not tell them what I was doing—leading to sin and guilt. I should have recognized that some of the things they asked about made sense for parents to know.

Several young people reported that they cringed at their parents' questions because they felt they could not live up to their parents' high expectations. They withheld information to avoid disappointing their parents and to avoid exposing themselves to powerful feelings of guilt. One young man explained how he hid his activities from his parents for this reason:

> Family rules were clear and fair. My parents expected a lot from me. They talked to me and showed interest in my activities and what was happening in my life. But they had such high expectations that many times I felt that it was better to hide things from them than face their disappointment.

Parents need to minimize hindrances to open

communication, including yelling and administering heavy-handed punishment when their teens disobey or make mistakes. It's difficult for teens to admit that they have not lived up to expectations or that they have broken family rules. To help teens overcome their fear of admitting their mistakes to their parents, Mom and Dad need to make confession as easy as possible. Teens need an opportunity to explain their actions and mention extenuating circumstances that may justify some parental clemency. If parents have shown understanding in the past, especially when the children were young, teenagers will find it easier to admit wrongdoing.

Our studies reveal that teens are willing to share information about their lives with their parents if they are asked in the right manner. Students surveyed resented too little interest as well as too much control. If parents ask questions in the right frame of mind and in the right situations, teens are generally willing to open up. The trick is for parents to determine the style of conversation that works best in helping a child share information.

One father discovered that when his sons started to date, the best information-gathering question was, "Do you have enough money?" It seemed less invasive than the typical when, where, what, and who questions. The sons viewed the question as an opportunity to squeeze a little extra cash out of dear old Dad, but unless they provided a little information about how, where, and on whom the money would be spent, Dad's cash stayed in his pocket. Once in a while the sons would be a little mysterious about where they were going, despite the money offer. At these times their father would half jokingly ask, "What if a good-looking girl calls for you? How will I know where to forward the call?" With that, the sons would laughingly reveal their plans for the evening.

Similar strategies work with daughters. If parents are interested and if they are willing to persevere and think of creative questions, they can usually keep track of their teenagers—and have some fun in the process.

Talk to the Right People

Children, particularly teens, hesitate to open up to their parents for a variety of reasons. They may fear that their parents will refuse to allow them to do something they really want to do, such as attend a special late-night party. They may be anxious that their parents will put a stop to some ongoing activity. They may not want to face their parents' disappointment or discipline should their parents become aware of their actions. As a consequence of these fears, youth sometimes blatantly lie, shade the truth, or withhold information. As a result, parents need a way to confirm the information teens volunteer about themselves.

During the Cold War, one of the slogans that guided negotiations between the United States and the former Soviet Union was "Trust but verify." This approach works well with parental monitoring. We can trust that our children, whatever their ages, are truthful with us regarding their friends, activities, behavior, school performance, money acquisitions and expenditures, and a host of other issues. But we need to know where to go to verify what they tell us.

One way to "trust but verify" is to seek information from our children's friends, parents of friends, teachers, Church leaders, and others who have contact with them. This isn't spying; it's parenting. It's not invading privacy; it's monitoring. Keeping our eyes wide open doesn't stop just at the front door. Our vigil doesn't end with the asking of a few questions.

When our children's friends come over, we can joke with them about what our son or daughter has told us concerning the group's activities. A funny look or blank stare should send up a red flag. Chance encounters with the parents of our children's friends may provide an opportunity to discuss teens and parenting. It's good news if the other parents are pleased with how their own children are behaving. Concerns about their children, however, may be a clue that something is going on that we may need to know about. If we rarely see the parents of our children's friends, we should call occasionally to find out how things are going.

Parents have many other sources of information that they can tap into with little effort. Coaches of athletic teams often have a sense for how children are doing. Music teachers, Church leaders and teachers, neighbors, and friends are also potential sources of information. These people have a pretty good idea about where your children's interests lie, and often they can provide a gauge of spiritual, social, and emotional well-being. These adults may even know of challenges or concerns that our children have not shared with us.

Parent-teacher conferences can give us information about how our children are doing in school. Information about participation in class discussions, homework assignments, respect for teachers, and interaction with others gives us a glimpse not only of their academic progress but also of other critical factors that may be affecting their lives.

If we're alert, our Heavenly Father helps us gather the information we need to know to effectively rear our children. That help can come in a variety of ways, but we must be ready to receive it by keeping our ears, eyes, and hearts wide open.

Watch for Warning Signs

In a garden, wilted or dried-out plants, half-eaten leaves, stunted growth, wormy vegetables, or flower blights send signals to the gardener that something is wrong and remedies are needed. Similarly, warning signs abound when it comes to our children. Some of these warning signs are pretty obvious: a pack of cigarettes in a backpack, empty beer cans in the family car, drug paraphernalia in a shirt pocket. Most warning signs, however, are not as obvious. Prolonged sadness, loss of interest in favorite activities, and excessive sleep or a lack of it can be signs of depression or emotional illness. Tardiness, missed classes, declining grades, and poor academic effort may signal that your teen's attention has shifted elsewhere.

Changes in a child's normal behavior are also signs that things may not be right. Staying out late at night, neglecting chores, and losing enthusiasm for the Church should elicit parental investigation. Personality changes, including increased moodiness and violent outbursts against brothers and sisters, may indicate drug abuse. Unusually picky eating habits, secretiveness about eating, and trips to the bathroom after meals may suggest a teenager is having trouble with bulimia or anorexia. Weepiness, withdrawal, or anger may indicate moral transgressions.

Adding new friends and dropping old friends usually signals that your child has become involved in a different social scene. Parents need to keep their eyes open to determine whether that scene includes support for gospel principles or greater temptations. The dress and manners of new friends offer a clue to the answer. Unfortunately, not all warning signs will be as obvious as clothing, tattoos, nose rings, or spiked hair.

One of the most reliable warning signs available to parents is the influence of the Holy Ghost. Sometimes we just have a gut feeling that something isn't right. When we receive promptings, we need to be more vigilant in monitoring our children and watching for less-obvious warning signs. If we are close enough to our children, we can tell when they have lost the Spirit.

While it is important that we keep our eyes wide open to warning signs, we must not close our eyes to positive signs. Performing in a school band, playing on a sports team, making the honor roll, and earning a Duty to God award or a Young Women medallion usually indicate that our son or daughter is making progress.

Keeping your eyes focused on activities, attitudes, and accomplishments is essential to rearing righteous and responsible children. Keeping your eyes wide open is essential for effective family instruction, as well as for family discipline. We need all the help we can get—especially the Lord's help—with these divine responsibilities. Someone once wisely observed, "Ninety percent of inspiration is information."

Being genuinely interested in your children's lives, being a hands-on parent by monitoring them, asking them lots of questions, gathering information from other people, and watching for warning signs gives you information that can help lead to vital inspiration. Most important, keeping your eyes wide open is an expression of your parental love and genuine concern and hopes for a happy and productive future for your children.

Note

1. Partnership for a Drug-Free America, "Keeping Tabs on Kids," www.drugfreeamerica.org.

Chapter 7

Dare to Discipline

♥

Years ago President Hugh B. Brown of the First Presidency recounted a story in general conference about a small currant bush pruned by a loving gardener. The bush, feeling that the pruning was unjust and unnecessary, cried out, "How could you be so cruel to me; you who claim to be my friend." The allegorical gardener responded:

> Do not cry; what I have done to you was necessary that you might be a prize currant bush in my garden. You were not intended to give shade or shelter by your branches. My purpose when I planted you was that you should bear fruit. . . . You must not weep; all this will be for your good; and some day, when you see more clearly, when you are richly laden with luscious fruit, you will thank me and say, "Surely, he was a wise and

loving gardener. He knew the purpose of my being, and I thank him now for what I thought was cruelty."[1]

President Brown used this story to illustrate that God's dealings with his children, although sometimes viewed by mortal men as cruel, are really acts of kindness and love designed to bring about our growth and happiness. Likewise, the discipline dispensed by caring and conscientious parents may be misunderstood and unappreciated by their children at the time. Parental discipline is, nonetheless, a loving act of kindness designed to protect, instruct, and bless our families.

Prior to the ninth grade, a young man in a family we know was a model son who attended Church regularly, excelled in his studies, and had many friends. During his teenage years, however, he became rebellious, dropped out of school, eventually developed a drug habit, and had numerous problems with the police and the courts. Because he was young, he was never really punished by the juvenile court system. He received several slaps on the wrist, was repeatedly placed on probation, and continued to fall back into his wild ways.

No matter what punishment his parents tried at home, they could not turn their son from his destructive lifestyle. Finally, when he was twenty years old and leading his younger brother down the same path, the courts, with help from the parents, threw the book at him. Two years' confinement in the state penitentiary changed his life. He stopped using drugs, completed his GED, and returned to activity in the Church. After his release he attended college, married in the temple, and is now living an exemplary life with his wife and children.

Unfortunately, not all young men and women who fall into similar situations see the error of their ways and return to the light of gospel living. Not all personal stories have happy endings. But the moral of the story is always the same: disobedience to rules and laws eventually results in punishment. At first the punishment may be subtle, such as teasing by friends and acquaintances or grounding and withholding of privileges by parents. Later in life the punishment may become more serious, such as being fired from a job or sent to prison. If parents don't teach their children that they will reap what they sow, they had better hope that teachers, friends, and Church leaders do.

Most parents want to have friendly, fun relations with their children, and they realize that disciplining them may, at least temporarily, sour their harmonious relationship. Although disciplining may be difficult for most parents, it is absolutely critical if children are to learn the important lesson that they are accountable for their actions and that actions have consequences.

Because imposing discipline, including punishments and restrictions, is emotionally exhausting, we sometimes wish someone else would do it for us. Wouldn't it be nice if each ward called an official "ward disciplinarian"? Perhaps the bishop could find a retired Army drill sergeant. Parents could send their disobedient youth to the ward meetinghouse one evening each week with a note concerning their misbehavior during the week. Then the ward disciplinarian could administer appropriate discipline. Fortunately, the responsibility to discipline children remains squarely on the shoulders of parents, where it belongs.

Several years ago as a bishop was conducting an interview with a brother who had recently moved into the ward, the new ward member admitted that he had been guilty of serious moral transgressions. He explained to the new bishop that he had confessed to his previous bishop and was now "ready to get a temple recommend." The bishop wasn't so sure, so he probed a little deeper to discern the man's level of repentance and conversion. "Did your previous bishop or stake president hold a disciplinary council for you?" he asked.

"No," the man responded. "He didn't do anything other than just to tell me not to do it again."

"Why wasn't any discipline administered?" the bishop asked.

The young man declared, "He was a *loving* bishop, not a *disciplining* bishop."

His reply revealed his misunderstanding of both words—*love* and *discipline.* He viewed them as mutually exclusive, when in reality they go hand in hand. Where there is love there must also be discipline. The scriptures repeatedly remind us that those whom God loves, he also chastens, or disciplines (Hebrews 12:6; Mosiah 23:21; Helaman 12:3; D&C 95:1).

Just as the young man misunderstood what discipline really means and how it relates to love, we often do the same when we think of discipline only in terms of *punishment.* The word *discipline* means to teach, guide, lead, direct, instruct, correct, and *chasten,* which means "to make pure."[2] Punishment is a part of discipline but only one component of a process by which we teach and lead our children in paths of righteousness and responsibility. When we view our stewardship this way, we can see more clearly our obligation to discipline our children, not despite or separate from our love for them, but *because* we love them.

Parental Discipline among Latter-day Saints

This issue of family discipline and its relationship to the emotional closeness as well as the religious training of Latter-day Saint families has been a prominent feature of our research through the years.

We were curious about what behaviors precipitate discipline or punishment in LDS families, so we asked the high school students in our survey sample to identify the behaviors. In addition, we asked hundreds of BYU students to identify the behaviors or activities for which their parents punished them while they were in high school. The list compiled from high school and college students is familiar to parents of teens. The descriptive statistics, coupled with insightful comments from the youth about parental discipline, provide an interesting picture from which important lessons can be learned.

Common Reasons for Disciplining Teens

Not surprisingly, staying out too late, violating family curfew, or failure to call when late were the most frequently cited behaviors drawing parental discipline. Parents know that teens (and preteens) who are out too late at night are at far greater risk for a variety of temptations and dangers, both physical and spiritual.

One young man reported that his parents disciplined him for "staying out after my established curfew, but most important, for not calling if I was going to be late." A young woman said she was disciplined for "lying about my whereabouts and staying out past curfew." Another said:

> Staying out too late (past curfew) is worthy of extensive punishment. Most of all, deceiving my

parents elicits the greatest punishment. Telling them I would be one place and then going someplace else is bad.

Though they didn't agree with their parents, most of the students acknowledged that their parents disciplined them to teach them to return to the safety of their home at a reasonable hour.

Arguing and fighting among brothers and sisters was the second most frequently mentioned behavior that led to parental discipline. Parents discipline children who fight because fighting not only disrupts family life but also poses a serious challenge to a reverent gospel atmosphere in the home.

Disrespect for parents, such as sassing or talking back, was number three on the discipline list. One young man reported, "My parents really got upset when I sassed them or talked back to them." A young woman said she got into serious trouble for showing disrespect. "Smart back talk or sassing is not allowed in our home," she said.

A number of high school and college students reported that they were disciplined for not doing assigned chores. A young woman said, "When I 'forgot' to do my assigned work around the house, my parents would usually ground me or take away some privilege." A young man replied, "My parents feel that my not doing my chores is a serious thing and will usually discipline me."

It probably isn't the dirty dishes or shaggy lawn

that irritates parents so much as the lack of responsibility demonstrated by their teenager. Discipline is necessary to reinforce the importance of keeping commitments.

Students only infrequently mentioned school problems such as skipping class, not completing homework, misbehaving in class, and making poor grades. These behaviors were identified as common reasons for discipline because parents view them as serious breaches of family rules. The frequency that LDS teens engaged in them influenced their position on the list. Staying out past curfew is a serious concern to parents and yet is something teens really enjoy, so they ignore curfew quite often. On the other hand, disrespect toward parents and unacceptable school performance are probably considered pretty serious but appeared lower on the list.

Common Forms of Punishment

Three out of four students said their parents use some form of grounding as their main disciplinary tactic. Parents usually prohibit their teens from going out in the evening or on weekends, which to most teens is a fate worse than death. Sometimes parents restrict access to the family car. Some parents curtail such privileges as watching television, listening to music, or talking on the phone. Others increase work assignments around the house.

One young man observed:

> They did not punish too severely. They rarely hit or even yelled. Instead, they punished in ways they knew would really affect me: grounding me, not allowing me to go on dates, and giving me an early curfew.

A young woman added:

> They give me the usual lecture about responsibility and then ground me for the weekend or have me wash dishes extra nights besides my turn (which they rarely follow through on) or ground me from reading my novels.

Half of the students surveyed reported that their parents yell at them, which they resent and feel is counterproductive. One young man reported:

> My dad yelling at me is the only thing that I really did not like growing up. I still have a lot of bitter feelings and resentment for things my dad said in anger that continue to hurt me to this day.

A young woman complained:

> I wish they didn't yell at me and break things when they are angry with me. I wish they didn't criticize us in front of others.

Another replied:

> My mom yells when she gets upset with something I do, which I do not like. I feet it shows a lack of self-control on her part.

About 5 percent of the teens indicated that their parents use psychologically controlling behaviors, such as withdrawing their love and creating excessive guilt feelings in them. One young man said the guilt trips are worse than other punishment:

> Mostly it is just that my dad will not let tensions die for a few days. So I feel miserable and don't want to do things that will cause him to act that way.

A young woman reported a similar experience:

> The hard punishment by parents is they make me feel guilty! I just feel that if I do something wrong my parents will stop loving me. Even though they have never stopped loving me, the guilt trips make me feel this way.

Another said:

> Dad would get upset and not say anything but would give me looks that could pierce anyone's heart. Sometimes he would say that he was disappointed in me (which was worse than hitting).

Occasionally parents express their disappointment by refusing to look at or talk to a child. A later chapter will discuss the negative consequences that psychologically controlling disciplinary techniques have on the emotional development of young people.

Another 5 percent of the young people said they

were hit, slapped, or spanked by their parents. Young adult students expressed resentment about their parents' use of corporal punishment, which sometimes bordered on abuse. A young man said:

> I did not like being punished with a Ping-Pong paddle or cayenne pepper. Sometimes our house was very contentious, and the yelling, fighting, swearing, and other types of punishment were not what I wish had happened.

A young woman gave a similar response:

> It wasn't often that my parents spanked me or used a belt to whip me. But these incidences were always ugly, always brought out the worst in everyone, and replaced love and respect with fear and disdain.

A young man said:

> I would change my parents' corporal punishment. Both my parents believe in spanking. This made me scared of them when I was little. It definitely made me scared of my father. I have resolved to find alternative means of punishing my own children.

Physical punishment can be an effective means of controlling behavior, but it creates fear and other strong emotions in youth that tend to persist into adulthood. A swat on the seat of a young child may be appropriate, but whipping a teenager with a belt raises serious concerns and borders on abuse.

Reactions of Teens to Discipline

Finally, we asked the students whether they felt the punishment they received was generally fair and fit the infraction of which they were guilty. More than 85 percent acknowledged that their parents were fair in their discipline. A comment from a young man was typical:

> My dad and mom are very fair in their discipline of me. They make sure I am guilty; they give me a chance to explain my side. Their punishment usually is reasonable for what I have done. I am not punished very often, and when I am, I deserve it.

Many students realize that their parents punish them out of love and concern for their welfare. One young woman wrote:

> I have come to know how hard it is to punish the ones you love. My parents let me know all the time that they wish they didn't have to take away privileges.

On the other hand, a few young people complained that their parents are too strict or that they play favorites with certain siblings. Some parents appear to be overly concerned about controlling their children, dictating too many rules about rather inconsequential behaviors. One youth complained:

My parents are too strict, and I am not allowed to do things that other kids my age could do. I am punished for things that just do not seem fair!

Much to our surprise, more youth wished that their parents had disciplined them more often and more severely than those who complained of too much discipline! A young man reported:

Often I felt I should have been punished for some of the things I did. I often felt I was not cared about because I was not punished for anything. I also had no rules or chores. I felt that my parents just didn't care what I did, which in many instances they didn't. They were too wrapped up in their own lives.

A young woman revealed the same feeling:

I think my mom should have punished me more, maybe by grounding because I was never grounded in my life. She should have taken away a privilege in order for me to learn a lesson. I was never really punished in my life.

Another teen said:

My parents should have stuck to their punishment. They always let me off the hook early. I think it would have been more effective if they wouldn't have done that.

Dos and Don'ts of Effective Discipline

From our studies and personal experiences have emerged several principles of effective discipline. We have tried to articulate the principles in the form of some helpful suggestions for parents. We hope these practical suggestions will help parents provide the guidance youth need within a context of love and concern and that these ideas will help transform discipline from an emotionally laden battle between parent and child to an accepted part of growing up—an expression of parental love and respect. These principles seemed to be universal among the parents who were most effective in raising righteous and responsible children. The actual methods, however, were quite diverse.

Our Heavenly Father sometimes sends drastically different spirits into the same family—not to watch us struggle but to remind us that our children are unique individuals and must be reared accordingly. As you read these suggestions or principles, we hope you will think deeply about how you can apply them in your home and that you will seek the Spirit in doing so.

Continual Maintenance Prevents Major Repairs

One of the most interesting things to emerge from our analysis of statistics concerning disciplining teens was the seeming lack of severe discipline or what might be seen as major blowups in the most effective families. More than two-thirds of the teens in our studies reported that they were punished by their parents only two or three times a year. Was it because these teens never disobeyed family rules, defied their parents, or did dumb things? Were they just naturally more righteous than other teens? Probably not.

Our research shows that LDS youth, generally, face the same challenges, are exposed to the same temptations, and feel the same emotional insecurities and vulnerabilities as adolescents everywhere. Likewise, LDS parents, regardless of geography, language, or culture, face the same daunting task of raising righteous children in a wicked world.

So what makes the difference in homes where there seems to be little need for severe punishment? As a rule, parents who clearly establish family rules, monitor their children's behavior, and consistently administer what could be called "maintenance discipline" have far fewer needs for major discipline.

For example, if a car owner never or rarely changes the oil in his vehicle or disregards the service engine warning light, he will inevitably have a major breakdown. He will have to pay hundreds, perhaps thousands, of dollars to repair or replace the engine—an expense that could have been averted by regular servicing of his car. Regular oil changes are relatively inexpensive, especially when compared to buying a new engine.

In families, consistent maintenance checks— establishing and periodically evaluating family rules, monitoring children's behavior, and letting consequences follow—will eliminate or at least reduce "breakdowns" and the need for major discipline.

Discuss the Reasons for Discipline

The Book of Mormon prophet Alma declared that God gave Adam and Eve "commandments, *after having made known unto them the plan of redemption*" (Alma 12:32; emphasis added). The commandments make sense when the plan of salvation is understood. The pattern established by our Heavenly Father works the same way in our families. Discipline has a greater impact in the life of a child when the child understands why he is being disciplined.

Parents need to move beyond "I am the parent, that's why" to reasonable explanations of family rules, their hopes and aspirations for their children, and how obedience will help children become all they can be. Youth need to know that a curfew should be kept because they are more at risk to dangers such as drinking, drugs, immorality, and other forms of delinquency during the late-night hours.

Too often parents discipline a child in a burst of anger because they feel their authority has been challenged. In anger and frustration, they are hardly in a position to help the youth understand the reasons for discipline or to teach how the discipline is tied to an important principle. Parents must control their anger, and whether by essays, discussions, or father's interviews, they need to clearly spell out what their child did wrong and why the rule is important to the child, the family, the Church, and God.

One young man stated:

> Teens should be told what they have done wrong, be given a reasonable explanation of why that was important, and then be given a reasonable punishment.

Another young man said:

> My parents make me write essays when I get in trouble on why I shouldn't do what I did. This form of punishment teaches me the "why" behind obedience.

Sometimes, however, no matter how reasonable or frequent the explanations, our children will still say things like, "Why not?" or "Give me thirteen good reasons." When this happens, it is usually clear that they are not asking for greater understanding but rather are expressing their disagreement with parental expectations or discipline. In these circumstances, no amount of reasoning with them will work. They want what they want. So after we have clearly explained the reasons for the rules and the discipline, we may just have to end the discussion with the words of newsman Walter Cronkite: "That's the way it is."

Make the Punishment Fit the Crime

Parents need to reserve serious punishment for serious offenses and mete out lighter punishment for minor offenses. A young man in our study stated:

> My parents punished us too severely—they yelled and spanked. They should have punished us in other ways, such as taking away privileges like dating and late curfews. They punished everything we did—no matter how bad it was—with exactly the same harsh punishment.

A young woman expressed similar sentiments:

> We were punished harshly for little things, which didn't seem fair. We felt like we should do the big things since we received the same punishment.

Decide what is important to your family, what rules matter the most, and what offenses should carry the harshest consequences. Then render punishment accordingly. In one family, violating curfew brings more serious punishment than neglecting chores. One teenage girl stated:

> In my family, we are punished more severely when we lie than when we just disobey. From that, we all know that lying just makes matters worse and that honesty really is the best policy.

If the rules are fair, the consequences clearly stated, and the principles adequately explained, then discipline must naturally follow. We must not back down. If we are doing what is right, we must stand our ground and let the consequences follow. To do otherwise sends the wrong signals, teaches the wrong lessons, and undermines the very foundations of righteousness and responsibility upon which we are seeking to build our homes.

Say What You Mean and Mean What You Say

Several studies in the past few decades have shown that when parents fail to consistently discipline inappropriate behavior, young people become confused about what is right and what is wrong. Being consistent is time-consuming and requires emotional stability. At times frazzled parents are willing to overlook an infraction to broker a little peace. At other times they explode because they are frustrated with work, a cranky baby, or a car that won't start. Such lapses create uncertainty in children.

One of the teenagers we interviewed described the confusion he experienced from his parents' haphazard discipline:

> My parents have a major problem with discipline. They never set unified, concrete rules. One thing is like okay with Dad but not with Mom. Mom's rules change depending on her moods and the amount of sleep she got. I would appreciate their explaining to me what the rules and limits are so I won't be so angry when they "punish"

me for some rule I didn't think I had even disobeyed.

This young man was frustrated with his parents' inconsistencies, not their discipline. Another young man did not like the inconsistency in punishment his parents administered to different children:

> I did not like the way punishment was given. There was no one punishment for something. So if one child lied, they would receive one punishment; when somebody else lied, it was different.

Perceptions of favoritism can have devastating effects on a parent-child relationship and serious long-term consequences.

Surprisingly, the most frequent complaint about discipline involved parents not following through on discipline for violations of clearly understood rules. A young woman explained her parents' inconsistency:

> This may sound strange, but I look back and wish that my parents, especially my mom, would have disciplined me more! My mom has admitted that because she stepped in and "saved" me from discipline from my dad and from natural consequences of wrong behaviors that now I am learning things I should have learned a long time ago.

Another example illustrates how a father's inconsistency—even when he may have thought he was doing his daughter a favor—actually alienated rather than endeared her:

I would have had more respect for my parents if they had been more consistent in their disciplining of me. For instance, I recall that my dad repeatedly told me to do my job, the dishes, for the week. I kept putting them in the back of my mind, not wanting to do them. My dad gave up and did them himself. I remember being frustrated at him for not setting his foot down and demanding that I heed him despite the fact that I didn't want to do them.

A young man remembered:

My mom and dad would angrily say I was grounded for a week. But after one day they would forget, and I would go back to doing what I wanted. I wish they had followed up and made me serve out the grounding. I had to learn later that in other situations discipline is not forgotten.

A college-age young woman told a similar story:

My parents' disciplining skills are horrible! They give me a punishment and then don't do anything about it. Not punishing kids and protecting and shielding them from bad experiences caused by their bad choices undermine learning experiences necessary to life.

Once parents decree a punishment, they should spend the necessary time and energy to see that it is carried out. But they should not rashly pronounce punishments in the heat of battle when they are angry and frustrated.

Parents who lack the will, courage, or stamina to

enforce discipline undermine the very lessons regarding obedience and accountability they want their children to learn. This is not to say that occasionally a parent cannot praise a teenager for sincere contrition and shorten the grounding or lighten the punishment. But such occasions should be contingent on obvious and sincere evidence that the child has learned from his mistake and has resolved to do better.

Now that we have stressed consistency, we recognize that there may be times when parents must treat their children differently. Such *conscious inconsistency* is based on the principle of "unto whom much is given much is required" (D&C 82:3). For example, the rewards and discipline associated with academic performance may be different for a bright child as compared to an average child. Young people understand that some children have more ability than others and that it is not only okay but also expected that parents take this into account.

Another form of conscious inconsistency is for parents to recognize that what works for one child may not work for another. A young man reported:

> For me, spanking worked well, but for my younger sister, it did not, and she rebelled. I know my parents were trying to be consistent, but not all children can be disciplined the same way. They should have tried something different with my sister.

Parents should notice what works best with each child and then customize rules and their attached consequences. We can be true to the spirit of the law without having to follow the letter of the law in every situation and with every child. Interestingly, teens in our study overwhelmingly reported that they would accept conscious inconsistencies if they were reasonable and explained.

Lower Your Voices

As mentioned earlier, the young people in our research overwhelmingly disliked being yelled at by their parents. Yelling is the least effective form of punishment and is almost always emotionally destructive. It is not really discipline at all but rather the frustrated and angry expressions of "the natural man" (Mosiah 3:19). Yelling often instills fear and resentment, not instruction or motivation.

One young man reported:

> I wish my dad would have tempered his anger and not yelled so violently. It frightened me when he was angry and yelling physical threats.

A young woman noted:

> I hate it when my folks yell at me. I know I have done wrong and am ready to pay the penalty. Their yelling makes the situation so much more painful, it is scary.

It is natural for parents to become emotional

when they discover that their children have done wrong things. But parents with bad tempers or a propensity to act out emotionally should postpone confrontations with their children until they have cooled down. They would do well to follow one of Thomas Jefferson's rules of personal conduct: If irritated, count to ten before saying anything. If really irritated, count to one hundred.

When parents control their emotions, they can rationally explain their disappointment, listen to their teen's justification, and discuss appropriate discipline. This will make discipline more effective and certainly less stressful. "Let us lower our voices in our homes," President Gordon B. Hinckley has admonished parents and children.[3]

> We seldom get into trouble when we speak softly. It is only when we raise our voices that the sparks fly and tiny molehills become great mountains of contention. . . .
>
> How much greater the peace in the homes of the people, how much greater the security in the lives of the children, how much less divorce and separation and misery, how much more gladness and joy and love there would be if husbands and wives would cultivate the discipline of speaking softly one to another, and if both would so speak to their children.[4]

When those moments invariably occur that we forget to control our emotions and the volume of our voices, there is something we can do. As hard as it may be at the time, we need to say to our children, "I'm so sorry for losing my temper. Let's start over."

Avoid Physical Punishment

Substantial evidence in child development literature argues that corporal punishment, such as spanking, whipping, or beating, is actually counterproductive. Rather than being instructive discipline, it is often humiliating and induces fear and anger. The young people in our studies almost unanimously condemned corporal punishment. They weren't talking about a swat on the diaper-clad rear end of a toddler or young child, but rather the hitting, slapping, and beating of older children, teens, and even young adults. One young man said:

> My parents were terrible at disciplining us kids. They usually hit us, sometimes with a stick or belt. In my opinion spanking solves nothing. Spanking or hitting only occurs when parents lose control of their emotions. I will not spank my children as my parents did me.

A young woman reported:

> I hated my parents when they whipped me for something I did wrong. It was an ugly, angry experience. I harbored bitter feelings against my parents for a long time after each spanking. I know there are better ways to handle disciplinary issues.

Several youth noted that their parents had not hit them. A young man stated:

> I appreciate that I was never physically hit by my parents. When they were upset with my actions, they let me know that they were very disappointed, and that hurt worse than a whipping and made me want to please them.

A young woman added:

> My parents' discipline is just telling me how they are disappointed in my decision. It is the hardest, most heart-wrenching discipline ever. When a mother looks at you and you can see the disappointment in her eyes, nothing is more effective.

A swat on the rear end of a toddler or young child is a quick and easy way to teach the child acceptable and unacceptable behaviors. A body of scientific literature suggests that "non-abusive" spanking can be beneficial, as a last resort, when disciplining children ages two to six years old.[5] But physical punishment of older children, particularly teenagers, is usually far more emotionally charged and has been found to have long-term negative consequences.

A recent review of social science research about physical punishment strongly cautions against its use. Corporal punishment has been linked to anti-social behavior, restricted cognitive development in children, and violence in dating relationships. The author, a well-known social scientist, argues that we need a Surgeon General's warning against spanking similar to the one linking smoking to lung cancer.[6] He suggests that every birth-certificate carry the notice: "Warning: spanking has been determined to be dangerous to the health and well-being of your child." Grounding, withdrawing privileges and modest parental disapproval are better ways of disciplining teenagers.

President Hinckley has often recounted how his parents raised him without corporal punishment. It so impressed him that, as a parent, he did the same—using love, discussion, and natural consequences.

> I don't believe that children need to be beaten, or anything of that kind. Children can be disciplined with love. They can be counseled—if parents would take the time to sit down quietly and talk with them. Tell them the consequences of misbehaving, of not doing things in the right way. The children would be better off, and I think everyone would be happier.
>
> My father never touched us. He had a wisdom all his own of quietly talking with us. He turned us around when were moving in the wrong direction, without beating us or taking a strap to us or any of that kind of business. I've never been a believer in the physical punishment of children. I don't think it is necessary.[7]

Avoid Withdrawal of Love

As we have discussed earlier, there's a fine line between parental disapproval and the withdrawal of love and acceptance. But it is a line parents need to recognize so they can stay on the side of disapproval. The key is to simultaneously express love for your children and disappointment in their behavior.

It is appropriate for parents to express disappointment that a son or daughter came home two hours after curfew. But refusing to look at or talk to a teen probably crosses the line. Such behavior says, "I don't love you any more" or "I can't stand the sight of you."

A young woman reported:

> My mom had her own unique way to punish me. She would tell me to go to my room and that she did not want to even look at me or talk to me. Sometimes this silent treatment lasted two or three days.

Creating excessive guilt in a teen is a manifestation of love withdrawal, which is a form of psychological control. One young man explained:

> When I do something wrong, my parents make me feel really guilty, like I have done the worse thing possible. Their treatment of me makes me feel worthless and undeserving of their love. They give me terrible guilt trips.

Like the wise and loving gardener who pruned

his prized currant bush, we must dare to discipline our children. It is difficult, time-consuming, and draining. Sometimes it may even be met with opposition and misunderstanding. We may not always like doing it, but we will like much less the consequences that will inevitably come if we fail to do so.

The fruits of parental pruning are worth the effort, just as they were in President Hugh B. Brown's parable of the currant bush. Someday when our children are bearing fruit—fulfilling their life's dreams, raising their own righteous families, and basking in the warmth of a well-lived life—they will appreciate our pruning efforts and the deep love we expressed.

Notes

1. Hugh B. Brown, *Eternal Quest*, ed. Charles Manley Brown (Salt Lake City: Bookcraft, 1956), 243–45.

2. *Webster's New Dictionary of Synonyms* (Springfield, Mass.: G. & C. Merriam, 1973), 248.

3. Gordon B. Hinckley, "'An Humble and a Contrite Heart,'" *Ensign*, November 2000, 89.

4. Gordon B. Hinckley, *Teachings of Gordon B. Hinckley* (Salt Lake City: Deseret Book, 1997), 201.

5. Craig H. Hart, Lloyd D. Newell, and Lisa L. Sine, "Proclamation-Based Principles of Parenting and Supportive Scholarship," in *Strengthening Our Families: An In-Depth Look at the Proclamation on the Family*, ed. David C. Dollahite (Provo, Utah: Center for the Studies of the Family, Brigham Young University, 2000), 100–123; see also Robert E.

Larzelere, "A Review of the Outcomes of Parental Use of Nonabusive or Customary Physical Punishment," *Pediatrics,* vol. 98 (4 October 1996): 824–28.

6. Murray A. Straus, "New Evidence for the Benefits of Never Spanking," *Society,* vol. 38 (September/October 2001): 52–60.

7. "At Home with the Hinckleys," *Ensign,* October 2003, 26.

Chapter 8

Praise More than You Criticize

Anyone who grows a vegetable or flower garden knows the feeling of anticipating summer roses, vine-ripened tomatoes, or fresh-picked sweet corn. A gardener always has high hopes and expectations for a bounteous harvest. How silly it would be, then, for a gardener who has planted the best quality seeds or bedding plants and who has conscientiously watered and weeded to then spray a powerful herbicide on those plants.

A gardener could take such drastic action for several possible reasons. He could do so out of anger or frustration that his plants aren't growing as fast or blossoming as beautifully as his high expectations demand. "If my tomatoes are not blue-ribbon, grand prize winners, I will not have any," he could declare.

He could do so out of embarrassment that his garden isn't as beautiful as his neighbor's garden, and rather than not be the showcase of the subdivision he decides to replace his flower garden with gravel. He could do so inadvertently, spraying so much herbicide that his plants are adversely affected by his efforts to kill the weeds.

Unfortunately, some parents, like the gardener, "spray" a form of emotional herbicide on their children. They may do so for a variety of reasons and in a variety of ways—criticism, condemnation, picking at small faults and failures, or showing an unwillingness to forgive and forget. Whatever the means or motives, emotional herbicide always stunts the growth of our children, poisons our relationship, and reduces the harvest.

One of the most frequent complaints we heard from teens and young adults in our study dealt with the pressure they felt to live up to their parents' expectations and the criticism they received when they fell short. One young man stated:

> My parents have such high expectations for me, I feel like I can never measure up. They don't give me much credit for the good I do or how far I have come but are quick to point out when I fall short of their expectations for me.

There is nothing inherently wrong with having high expectations for our children. Our Heavenly Father has high expectations for his children. But his expectations are realistic, and he has provided the means whereby we are able to achieve those expectations. The teens and young adults of our study did not oppose or rebel against the high expectations of their parents. They clearly understood that parents want them to do right and to reach their potential, which is also what the youth want. They don't want to be slackers, nor do they want their parents to eliminate all expectations.

What bothers them, however, is when their parents have unrealistic expectations, when they're not content with anything less than top-of-the-class academic achievement, world championships in sports, and award-winning performances in the school play. Hundreds of youth in our study complained that high expectations often caused their parents to see only their shortcomings rather than their accomplishments. It seemed to them that Mom and Dad always saw the glass half empty instead of half full.

Nothing seems to discourage our children more than when parental expressions of criticism and displeasure, however well-intended, continually outnumber and overpower compliments and expressions of praise. Sometimes we parents don't even recognize our negativism because we are so intent on correcting our children and making sure they are on the right path. Sometimes we can't see the beautiful forest because we're distracted by two sickly, diseased trees. For example, a teenage girl in our study painfully observed:

> I get straight A's in high school, play on the soccer team, and am the Laurel president, but still my dad gets mad at me for not having dinner ready on time or all my chores done each day. He never sees that I go to seminary every morning, do well in school, go to soccer practice, practice piano, do all my homework—and some laundry. All he ever sees is what isn't done.

One young man mentioned how his father's constant criticism not only affected him as a young boy but also affects him today many years later:

> One of my responsibilities as a boy was to mow the lawn in the summertime. I didn't mind mowing the lawn, but I got so that I hated my dad's inspection of my work. He would point out any place that I had missed or if anything was not just perfect. No matter how hard I worked at it and no matter how good the job was that I had done, I could still expect criticism. The yard could be 99.9 percent perfect, but Dad would only comment on the .1 percent. It was never good enough.
>
> And it wasn't just mowing the lawn. It was like that with most everything. He would never say, "That looks great," or "You did a good job." He would only point out how I could have done things better. It made me feel like, "Why try?" Even now I feel like I can do nothing to please my father.

Undoubtedly, this father viewed his comments as

constructive criticism, void of malicious intent to emotionally harm his son or discourage his efforts. After all, it was his parental obligation to teach, guide, and correct. He thought he was doing what was right. But he did more harm than good.

When we think about all the things we need to teach our children, all the things we need to warn them about, all the things we need to encourage them to do, we can feel overwhelmed. Because none of our children is perfect, we could spend every moment correcting and criticizing them for something. Our children, who could probably spend all their time criticizing us and pointing out our parental faults, may feel that is exactly what we do. But not much good would come from that. Have you ever noticed that the more we get after our kids, the more we find to criticize? It's a vicious cycle.

We asked several hundred older parents whose children were already raised, "What do you wish you had done differently in rearing your children?" Many of them lamented that in their zeal to correct and counsel their children, they had been too quick to criticize the small things and too slow to praise the good things. Here are some of their comments:

> I wish I hadn't been so stressed out about every little thing that my kids did wrong. I was always getting after them. I was overly critical. As I look back now, I can see that most of the things that I got upset about and disciplined them for were really unimportant.

I wish now that I had been more willing to let the "small things" go without making a big deal about them. I was constantly nagging my children, and nothing good came from that.

Criticizing the kids was never helpful. It never solved the problem but only made things worse. I wish I hadn't learned that lesson the hard way.

I didn't use compliments enough or accentuate the positive. I focused too much on their negative behavior or the work that wasn't done, instead of looking for the good they did.

Several years ago President Gordon B. Hinckley observed, "We live in a society that feeds on criticism."[1] Unfortunately this ugly characteristic of modern society has manifested itself in all too many homes and families. Just as society is weakened and damaged by the trend to criticize and bash, so are our families. The hurt may not be quickly seen, but it is there and is slow to heal. President Hinckley's wise counsel has particular relevance to parents:

I am asking that we stop seeking out the storms and enjoy more fully the sunlight. I am suggesting that as we go through life we "accentuate the positive." I am asking that we look a little deeper for the good, that we still voices of insult and sarcasm, that we more generously compliment virtue and effort. I am not asking that all criticism be silenced. Growth comes from correction. Strength comes of repentance. Wise is the man who can acknowledge mistakes pointed out by others and change his course.

What I am suggesting is that each of us turn from the negativism that so permeates our society and look for the remarkable good among those with whom we associate, that we speak of one another's virtues more than we speak of one another's faults.[2]

There may be times when our children need constructive criticism. We would be wise if we view those moments as a wise doctor views medicine needed by an ailing patient. Even medicine can be a poison, so it must be administered in the correct dosage. An overdose can kill. So it is within the family context. Wise parents understand that the healthy prescription for righteous and responsible children is to curtail criticism and increase praise.

Accentuate the Positive

It is discouraging for anyone, but especially adolescents who naturally struggle with feelings of inadequacy, to feel as if nothing they do is ever good enough. Generous praise is a motivator. Buoyed up by praise rather than discouraged by a barrage of criticism, our children will try harder and do better. As the old adage goes, "You can catch more flies with honey than with vinegar." Praise is a form of positive reinforcement that really does improve behavior—not just of children but also of teens and adults. One young woman said:

One of the best things my parents did in raising us kids was to always praise and encourage us. Even if I drew an ugly picture at school, Mom would tell me how good it was and display it on the fridge. I knew it was ugly, but I was glad that Mom didn't tell me that. Her compliments and praise encouraged me to do better. Because of the praise we received, we wanted to please our parents, and that helped keep us out of trouble.

An environment of praise and encouragement opens our children to helpful correction and guidance. Criticism, on the other hand, often slams the door shut on improvement because it tends to put down rather than lift up—focusing on the negative rather than on the positive.

"Catch someone doing something good" is a slogan that educators often use. They understand that good behavior and proper attitudes will be forged more by praise and rewards than by criticism and punishment.

Several years ago a study examined the impact of different kinds of rewards for good schoolwork, such as putting together a puzzle. Successful students in one group received monetary rewards; those in a second group received verbal praise. Those who received verbal praise actually enjoyed their puzzles more and even spent free time working on them. The group that received monetary rewards quickly lost motivation and interest in the task. Interestingly, when students were criticized for unsatisfactory work, they lost motivation and reacted negatively to the task. Researchers found that praise was directly related to effort as well as to achievement.[3]

Expressions of praise, encouragement, and appreciation can work just as well, if not better, within our homes. We can suppress the natural parental urge to nag, criticize, and get after our children. Instead, we can catch them doing something good and praise them for it, no matter how small it may be. Looking for and recognizing something good our children do every day will not only help change their behavior but also change our behavior—and how we view them and feel about them.

At first, it may be difficult. But if we continue to work at it, the process will become easier because our children will be doing more good in response to our praise. "When children and teenagers are loved [and praised] because of who they are and not for how they behave, only then can we begin to help make much-needed changes in behavior," Elder H. Burke Peterson taught.[4] He suggested a way whereby parents can exhibit the love that will affect behavior:

> Look for the good in each person, and mention it in a sincere and consistent way. It is amazing how hearts can be softened, testimonies implanted, and relationships improved when we begin to give a daily portion of heartfelt appreciation. . . . Even mentioning a little thing will have

a positive effect. It usually isn't earth-shaking—just a simple act or attribute that will blossom and be multiplied if it is noticed. (By the way, it may take you all day to find something, but it is there.)[5]

Illustrating this important parental principle, Elder Peterson shared an experience from his family that demonstrates how accentuating the positive, even when it is difficult, yields better results than nagging and criticizing. His daughter and her family had made a goal to speak more positively to one another. They had also committed to look for the good and to encourage rather than condemn. Elder Peterson said:

> One day after school, one of our daughters came into a teenage son's room. It looked as if a big wind had blown through. He was sitting in the midst of it all. She felt the anger rising within, but remembered her resolution to look for the good. Searching desperately, her eye finally looked upward. "Your ceiling's really clean, Adam!" she was able to say quite honestly. He laughed; he got the message, and he cleaned up the room.[6]

Accentuating the positive through praise and encouragement (even if it requires complimenting a clean ceiling) is a great motivator. It is also a manifestation of charity—the pure love of Christ. Looking for the sunshine rather than remaining in the dark clouds of negativism and criticism allows us to realize that in life, as in families, there is far more sunlight than there are thunderstorms. Accentuating the positive will cause us to see our children in a new light—God's light. With this kind of divine illumination, we will see more clearly and love more deeply—and so will our children.

Forgive and Forget

"Behold, he who has repented of his sins, the same is forgiven, and I, the Lord, *remember them no more*" (D&C 58:42; emphasis added). This familiar passage in the Doctrine and Covenants is not only an important doctrinal declaration regarding the blessings of personal repentance and forgiveness but also an important principle for parents. How grateful we should be that the Lord remembers our sins no more, provided we repent of them.

Unfortunately, we sometimes aren't as merciful with our children as the Lord is with us. The comments from the young people in our study concerning their parents' apparent unwillingness to forgive and forget were almost as numerous as the comments about parents being overly critical and stingy with praise. Many of the teens and young adults said their parents would "hold things over my head" or "throw things back in my face," even many years after an event. Like criticism, the inability to forgive and forget discourages children and makes them feel that no matter what they do to "repent," they can never please their parents or regain their trust and approbation. One teen said:

> I hate it when my parents bring up things I have done in the past and hold them over my head, even though it may have been two years ago. It makes me feel so bad and that no matter how hard I try, they only remember the bad things.

Another added:

> Sometimes when I make mistakes my parents, especially my mother, throw back in my face things I did in the past. I thought they were over and done with, and yet they still bring them up. I don't know why they continue to do this other than to belittle me and make me feel terrible. Sometimes I just want to say, "Get over it!"

We need to remember what we want to accomplish. If we really want to change behavior, we should use the moments after our children have committed mistakes or made bad decisions as teaching moments for loving correction and proper discipline. Of course, we want to remind children not to continue making the same mistakes, but nothing good comes from repeatedly reminding them of their past misdeeds, especially when they haven't repeated those deeds.

Shortly after he had received his driver's license, one young man in our study had a minor fender bender while pulling the family car out of the garage. For years, every time he took the family car anywhere, his mother and father reminded him of that earlier accident. Perhaps they viewed their comments as a necessary caution or mere lighthearted teasing. Regardless, the son felt belittled, distrusted, and frustrated. His parents never expressed pride that he had never had another accident or that he had never received a speeding ticket, as had many of his friends. They never forgave or forgot.

Think how we would feel if, each time we made a mistake and tried to repent, our Heavenly Father said, "Yeah, but remember when you did this or that?" We would get so discouraged we would soon give up talking to God for fear of what might be thrown back in our face. Worst of all, we might give up trying to be righteous, feeling that no matter what we did, we would never be forgiven.

It is the love and mercy of the Lord—the knowledge that even with his omniscience, he can forgive and forget—that motivates us to try a little harder to be righteous and to keep repenting when we fall. It works the same with our children. Mercy, empathy, and genuine forgiveness, including a conscientious effort to forget and put the past behind us, are vital to the spiritual and emotional progress of our children. When we continually put them down because of past mistakes—even when our intent is to help them improve—we force them to emotionally and spiritually look back over their shoulders. When we are always looking backward, we can't effectively move forward.

Many years ago, President J. Reuben Clark Jr. of the First Presidency taught that when it comes to the Judgment, God "will give that punishment which is the very least that our transgression will justify. . . . I believe that when it comes to making the rewards for our good conduct, he will give us the maximum that it is possible to give."[7]

Parents should use this divine equation in dealing with their children. We can keep criticism and correction to a minimum and raise praise and commendation to new heights. We can show our children that the books are closed on past deeds. We can remember and remind less, and forgive and forget more.

Show Forth Increased Love

Several years ago a colleague conducted an experimental study of various styles of leadership and their effects. One of the styles of leadership he investigated was what could be characterized as "punitive leadership." This type of leader harshly punished when expectations were not met. Interestingly, a punitive leader got a great deal of work out of his subordinates. Productivity even increased—at least temporarily. But those who worked under the punitive leader began to greatly dislike him, resent his expectations and demands, and, ultimately, seek to escape his leadership.

The results of this study are not surprising. Common sense tells us that a tyrannical approach to leadership fosters fear, resentment, and rebellion. Beyond common sense, the revelations of God remind us that such a leadership style is antithetical to the spirit of the gospel of Jesus Christ. While incarcerated in Liberty Jail, the Prophet Joseph Smith received a profound revelation concerning leadership in general and priesthood or gospel leadership in particular:

> No power or influence can or ought to be maintained by virtue of the priesthood, only by persuasion, by long-suffering, by gentleness and meekness, and by love unfeigned; by kindness, and pure knowledge, which shall greatly enlarge the soul without hypocrisy, and without guile—
>
> Reproving betimes with sharpness, when moved upon by the Holy Ghost; *and then showing forth afterwards an increase of love toward him whom thou has reproved, lest he esteem thee to be his enemy; that he may know that thy faithfulness is stronger than the cords of death.* (D&C 121:41–44; emphasis added)

There is no greater gospel or priesthood leadership than that done within the context of the everlasting family. As parents, we must utilize these principles within the walls of our homes just as much, if not more, than do bishops and Relief

Society presidents at church. We are familiar with the charge to show increased love after discipline, but the phrase "lest he esteem thee to be his enemy" is vital to understanding why.

All of us have the natural urge to emotionally recoil when we have been chastened. We may feel a sting of hurt, disappointment, and maybe even some degree of embarrassment. Similarly, children, including teens, commonly feel somewhat rejected by their parents when they are disciplined. Because the behavior that elicited the discipline results in some form of disappointment (sometimes even anger) from Mom and Dad, it is quite common for children to feel emotionally estranged. For these reasons, it is vitally important for parents to reach out with expressions of increased love and acceptance.

Expressions such as "I love you no matter what" and "You mean the world to me," coupled with a warm hug or a tender arm around a shoulder, are probably more needed and will be more appreciated following discipline than at any other time. At these moments we need to *include* our children in the warmth of the family circle, not *isolate* them from it.

It will take work, practice, and a conscientious and continual effort to resist the urges of the natural man. No doubt it will be difficult to show increased love at certain times. But those are the very times that we should hug our children, tell them how much we love them, and remind them of how glad we are that they are ours. Only in this way will our children know that our "faithfulness is stronger than the cords of death."

Comments from youth and experienced parents alike illustrate how important this concept is to the emotional and spiritual welfare of family relationships. One young man recalled a rather humorous way his father combined love with discipline:

> When I was eight or nine years old I got into a pretty good fight with my older sister. I chased her down the hall, and she locked herself in the bathroom. I was so mad that I pounded on the door and then kicked it. My foot smashed a big hole in the door. My mom was pretty upset with the fight, but that really sent her through the roof. She sent me to my room and told me that when Dad got home he would punish me. A while later I heard Dad come home and talk to Mom. In a few minutes I heard him coming down the hall to my room. I knew I was in for it then.
>
> He came into my room holding a board and said, "You know you did wrong and now you have to be punished. Take it like a man." I had had spankings before but never with a board. So I was pretty scared. I leaned over the bed and braced myself. He swatted me with what I thought was a board, but instead it was a piece of Styrofoam. It promptly shattered into little pieces, and my father burst out laughing.
>
> As soon as I got over the initial shock, I started to laugh too. He then told me I would be

grounded and have to pay for the damage but that he and Mom loved me and hoped I would try harder to get along with my sister. I knew I had done wrong and needed to be punished, but this practical joke (which was Dad's way of dealing with a bad situation), combined with expressions of love and forgiveness, had a far greater impression on me than any form of discipline could have. I wanted to be better because of that.

A grandmother whose children are raised recalled the feelings of hurt, humiliation, and anger she felt when she received a phone call from the police, informing her that her teenage daughter had been arrested for shoplifting at the local mall. A million thoughts raced through her mind: *How could she do such a thing? She is going to be grounded for the rest of her life! I am such a failure as a mother.*

Her first impulse when she came face-to-face with her daughter was to chew her out and lower the boom of discipline. She sensed, however, that her daughter's feelings of humiliation, remorse, and disappointment—disappointment with herself and knowing that she had deeply disappointed and hurt her parents—were even deeper than the mother's feelings of anger, embarrassment, and humiliation. Profound feelings of love and compassion flooded over this wise mother as she put her arms around her daughter and expressed her love, forgiveness, and support. "We'll help you get through this," the mother said.

The mother's expressions of love and support didn't eliminate the need for punishment. The love just made the punishment more effective. "It wasn't as hard to do as you would think," the mother remembered. "I put myself in her place and thought about how much I would need love and reassurance of my worth." The punishment that followed that expression of love at that difficult time was far more effective in shaping immediate behavior and building long-term character.

President Brigham Young taught, "If you are ever called upon to chasten a person, never chasten beyond the balm you have within you to bind up."[8] Chastening is the work of parenthood. Unfortunately, many assume the word *chasten* only means *punish*. To chasten is "to make pure," "to refine," or "to correct for the purpose of reclaiming from evil."[9] The scriptures testify that God chastens those he loves (D&C 95:1). Likewise, parents can best chasten—refine, correct, purify, and instruct—when love abounds.

We can apply the balm of chastening love to our children by praising more than criticizing, accentuating the positive, forgiving and forgetting, and showing increased love when we must discipline. As we do, we will see a bounteous harvest not only in how our children *behave* but also in what they *become.*

Notes

1. Gordon B. Hinckley, "Five Million Members—A Milestone and Not a Summit," *Ensign*, May 1982, 46.

2. Gordon B. Hinckley, "The Continuing Pursuit of Truth," *Ensign*, April 1986, 4.

3. "Does Praise Help?" *Ensign*, March 1973, 48.

4. H. Burke Peterson, "Preparing the Heart," *Ensign*, May 1990, 83.

5. Ibid.

6. Ibid.

7. J. Reuben Clark Jr., "'As Ye Sow . . . ,'" *Speeches of the Year* (Provo, Utah: Brigham Young University, 3 May 1955), 7.

8. Brigham Young, in *Journal of Discourses*, 26 vols. (London: Latter-day Saints' Book Depot, 1854–86), 9:124–25.

9. *Webster's New Dictionary of Synonyms* (Springfield, Mass.: G. & C. Merriam, 1973), 248.

Chapter 9

Counsel but Don't Control

$\heartsuit$

Just as the gardener hopes his tender plants develop properly and ultimately yield an abundant harvest of beautiful and fragrant flowers or delicious fruits and vegetables, all parents pray that their efforts at home will yield a rich harvest: children who mature into righteous and responsible young adults, who have sufficient manners to be acceptable in society, and who adopt beliefs and values that foster achievement in school, success in a career, and happiness and fulfillment in family life.

Most parents would love to be able to transfer their own set of guiding principles, developed through the years from both bitter and sweet experiences, to their teenage children. But young people must internalize their own beliefs, values, and ideas.

Physical maturation, life experiences, influences of trusted friends and teachers, coupled with loving parental guidance, all contribute toward making teenagers who they are.

In this chapter we offer suggestions as to how parents can maximize their influence on their teenager's emerging personality. One of the most important things parents can do to foster maturity is to help their teen develop emotional independence. The most competent and righteous young adults have developed, with aid from the influences mentioned above, their own beliefs, values, and guiding principles. With this development comes a self-confidence that helps them make decisions.

Social scientists call the process whereby teenagers develop their set of beliefs about the world, their values of right and wrong, and their feelings about themselves *psychological autonomy.* This form of intellectual and emotional—not behavioral—independence is critical if young people are to successfully face decisions in daily life without Mom and Dad.

The young man or young woman who lives life by always asking for parental advice will be severely handicapped as a young adult and beyond. "Dad, do I like engineering or social science?" "Mom, tell me whether to accept a date from Fred, who doesn't share our beliefs or values?" Young adults need to be equipped to make good decisions on their own that will bring them happiness.

When Joseph Smith was asked how he governed the rapidly expanding membership of the Church, he replied with these famous words: "I teach them correct principles and let them govern themselves."[1] Despite this credo, Joseph was not totally successful in fostering psychological autonomy in all members of the Church. Many had not internalized gospel principles, relying too much upon the Prophet— being emotionally connected to him, culturally converted, or merely socially attached to Nauvoo. As a result, they died spiritually when the Prophet died physically.

So it is with us. We must teach our children correct principles and help them internalize those principles so they can successfully govern themselves. Sometimes we have difficulty allowing, let alone encouraging, our children to develop their own opinions, beliefs, and values. We sometimes fear that they will make mistakes, develop different ideas or opinions, or not become what we want them to be. Our children sometimes come up with weird ideas, opinions, and feelings that shock us.

We need to understand that it takes time for most adolescents to internalize what they have been taught and then develop their own mature set of acceptable beliefs and values. It doesn't happen automatically. It's all part of the maturing process—

physically, intellectually, emotionally, and spiritually. Preparing for adulthood is a process, not an event. Growing up comes as teens learn how to *become* mature spiritually and emotionally, not just by reaching the legal age of twenty-one.

We know that we must let go of our children someday—that they must leave the nest, establish their own emotional identities, live the gospel on their own, and have their own families. Hesitancy and failure to let go can become corrosive if not checked and can lead to dangerous psychological control. Parents manifest this kind of control in a variety of ways, but it is always a form of manipulating children's thoughts, opinions, and feelings rather than encouraging them to develop their own.

Without their own psychological autonomy, young people are ill equipped to deal with the real world. Several comments from young people in our studies illustrate this potential danger. One young man said:

> My parents are extremely controlling. They always had a say in everything I did. So now that I am older, it's hard to make any decision without asking my parents what I should do.

A young adult woman echoed these sentiments:

> I didn't like the fact that my parents didn't give me much agency when I was growing up. They told me what to think and how to act and forced me to do it. When I got on my own and

was faced with decisions, I didn't know how to make correct ones.

Psychological Autonomy vs. Behavioral Autonomy

Although related, psychological autonomy and behavioral autonomy are different. Parents often confuse the two. Teens show behavioral autonomy by behaving appropriately without being told what to do. Teens develop psychological autonomy when they form their *own set of internalized values that guide their behavior.* Thoughts, ideas, perceptions, and feelings are much easier to hide from parents than behavior, so parents must make extra effort to get their children to share them.

In surveys of several hundred LDS parents about what had worked for them in raising their children to adulthood, none mentioned shaping the thoughts, values, ideas, beliefs, perceptions, or feelings of their children. Their focus was on behavior, especially setting rules, monitoring obedience, and administering appropriate discipline. Shaping behavior is important, but it is only part of the task of transforming teenagers into righteous young adults. *Becoming requires more than just doing.*

As we have discussed at great length in previous chapters, our children need rules, monitoring, and discipline to guide their behavior and to help them understand foundational values and principles upon which their decisions must be based. Rules, choices, consequences, and discipline not only provide *behavioral control* but also establish the parameters in which *behavioral autonomy* can be freely given. Behavioral influences are positive and can be important blessings in the lives of our children as they mature. On the other hand, a lack of psychological autonomy—needed for *psychological control*—has devastating effects in the lives of young people.

Negative Consequences of Psychological Control

Considerable research during the past several decades has shown that adolescents who are denied psychological autonomy, and who have not developed their emotional identities because of parental psychological control, exhibit a number of undesirable behaviors. Teens who are psychologically controlled by their parents have lower grades in high school and are less likely to attend college. Even more important than its impact on academic achievement and career preparation, a lack of psychological autonomy has been found by numerous studies to be directly related to depression in teenagers and young adults.

Unfortunately, this phenomenon is manifesting itself at younger and younger ages—now seen in elementary and junior high schools. Emotionally and psychologically controlled kids feel that they simply cannot cope with the world in which they live. *Suicide ideation,* or thinking about committing suicide, is also a consequence of retarded autonomy. Eating disorders, bulimia, and anorexia appear more often among young people (particularly young women) denied psychological autonomy.

Finally, young people who lack psychological autonomy also tend to be more sexually promiscuous than those who have been reared in a healthy environment of psychological autonomy. Lack of psychological autonomy negatively affects both genders, but young women seem to suffer the effects more so than young men. The link between psychological autonomy and feelings about the self are obvious. Teens' feelings of self-worth, self-reliance, and self-confidence are significantly reduced by psychological control and emotional manipulation. In contrast, fostering psychological autonomy produces positive effects—increased self-worth, self-reliance, self-confidence, and fortified values and principles of character that have been taught at home and at Church.

Psychological autonomy can endow young people with appropriate views, beliefs, and values, as well as with high expectations and a gospel context that guides behavior. The psychologically autonomous are able to successfully function in society. Psychological autonomy and emotional independence empower our children and open the door to limitless possibilities. Stifling autonomy, by contrast, often slams that door shut and creates such an emotional fear in our children that they do not dare open it. One young woman from Great Britain praised her mother for helping her develop her own sense of emotional independence:

> My mum doesn't dictate, but she made sure I knew and respected her values. Now that I live on my own, her values have become my values too.

Similarly, a young man expressed appreciation to his parents for teaching him to make his own decisions based on his own values:

> They encouraged me to pursue my dreams without qualifying exactly what the dreams had to be. They instilled in me a real sense of independence so that when I moved out on my own, I wasn't calling home every five minutes wondering what to do next. I was guided by my own values. They had taught me those principles and values, but now they had become my own.

From our research and experiences we have discovered some practical things that parents can do to foster an environment that strikes a healthy balance between behavioral autonomy and psychological autonomy.

Nurturing Psychological Autonomy

Helping teenagers become psychologically independent is not difficult, but it requires patience and love unfeigned. While we primarily focus our suggestions for developing that independence in teenagers, it is important to realize that younger children also need to learn to develop their own thoughts, opinions, feelings, and values.

If we fall into a pattern of psychologically controlling our children when they are young, we won't all of sudden fall out of that pattern when they get older. A six-year-old can be as damaged by psychological control as a sixteen-year-old. The specifics may differ depending on the ages of our children, but the principles are basically the same.

Don't Withdraw Love or Induce Guilt

The first suggestion for fostering psychological independence is a *"thou shalt not."* Most parents discover that withdrawing love and inducing feelings of guilt are effective ways to control the behavior of their children. But children, particularly teenagers, would rather take a beating or lose privileges than have their parents withdraw their love, acceptance, and association.

Young people's aversion to this form of emotional manipulation can be seen in such statements as "I hated their guilt trips," "My mother is the queen of guilt trips," and "My dad gives the worst guilt trips."

One young man recognized the destructive consequences of the guilt induction his parents used on him and even now, much to his chagrin and disappointment, he finds himself using the same tool against his wife and children.

> I didn't like the guilt-trip method of discipline that my dad would use. It is effective, but I don't believe it helps a child really choose the right or learn from decisions. I wish he hadn't done the guilt trip thing because I've picked it up from him. I use it without even knowing that I've used it. I know it isn't a good teaching method.

Guilt induction and love withdrawal may be highly effective in controlling behavior in the short term, but they have devastating long-term consequences on young people's feelings about themselves and their abilities to manage their lives. One young man said, "Sometimes their discipline was to use guilt instead of grounding or loss of privileges. It was effective but made me feel really bad about myself."

Several years ago, Elder Jeffrey R. Holland recounted in general conference a dream he had had after disciplining his young son and sending him to bed without his customary bedtime story, prayer, hug, and kiss. His poignant story illustrates the damaging effects of love withdrawal.

> Early in our married life my young family and I were laboring through graduate school at a university in New England. Pat was the Relief Society president in our ward, and I was serving

in our stake presidency. I was going to school full time and teaching half time. We had two small children then, with little money and lots of pressures. In fact, our life was about like yours.

One evening I came home from long hours at school, feeling the proverbial weight of the world on my shoulders. Everything seemed to be especially demanding and discouraging and dark. I wondered if the dawn would ever come. Then, as I walked into our small student apartment, there was an unusual silence in the room.

"What's the trouble?" I asked. "Matthew has something he wants to tell you," Pat said. "Matt, what do you have to tell me?" He was quietly playing with his toys in the corner of the room, trying very hard not to hear me. "Matt," I said a little louder, "do you have something to tell me?"

He stopped playing, but for a moment didn't look up. Then these two enormous, tear-filled brown eyes turned toward me, and with the pain only a five-year-old can know, he said, "I didn't mind Mommy tonight, and I spoke back to her." With that he burst into tears, and his entire little body shook with grief. A childish indiscretion had been noted, a painful confession had been offered, the growth of a five-year-old was continuing, and loving reconciliation could have been wonderfully underway.

Everything might have been just terrific— except for me. If you can imagine such an idiotic thing, I lost my temper. It wasn't that I lost it with Matt—it was with a hundred and one other things on my mind. But he didn't know that, and

I wasn't disciplined enough to admit it. He got the whole load of bricks.

I told him how disappointed I was and how much more I thought I could have expected from him. I sounded like the parental pygmy I was. Then I did what I had never done before in his life—I told him that he was to go straight to bed and that I would not be in to say his prayers with him or to tell him a bedtime story. Muffling his sobs, he obediently went to his bedside, where he knelt—alone—to say his prayers. Then he stained his little pillow with tears his father should have been wiping away.

If you think the silence upon my arrival was heavy, you should have felt it now. Pat did not say a word. She didn't have to. I felt terrible!

Later, as we knelt by our own bed, my feeble prayer for blessings upon my family fell back on my ears with a horrible, hollow ring. I wanted to get up off my knees right then and go to Matt and ask his forgiveness, but he was long since peacefully asleep.

My relief was not so soon coming; but finally I fell asleep and began to dream, which I seldom do. I dreamed Matt and I were packing two cars for a move. For some reason his mother and baby sister were not present. As we finished I turned to him and said, "Okay, Matt, you drive one car and I'll drive the other."

This five-year-old very obediently crawled up on the seat and tried to grasp the massive steering wheel. I walked over to the other car and started the motor. As I began to pull away, I looked to see how my son was doing. He was trying—oh, how he was trying. He tried to reach the pedals, but he couldn't. He was also turning knobs and pushing buttons, trying to start the motor. He could scarcely be seen over the dashboard, but there staring out at me again were those same immense, tear-filled, beautiful brown eyes. As I pulled away, he cried out, "Daddy, don't leave me, I don't know how to do it. I am too little." And I drove away.

A short time later, driving down that desert road in my dream, I suddenly realized in one stark, horrifying moment what I had done. I slammed my car to a stop, threw open the door, and started to run as fast as I could. I left car, keys, belongings, and all—and I ran. The pavement was so hot it burned my feet, and tears blinded my straining effort to see this child somewhere on the horizon. I kept running, praying, pleading to be forgiven and to find my boy safe and secure.

As I rounded a curve nearly ready to drop from physical and emotional exhaustion, I saw the unfamiliar car I had left Matt to drive. It was pulled carefully off to the side of the road, and he was laughing and playing nearby. An older man was with him, playing and responding to his games. Matt saw me and cried out something like, "Hi, Dad. We're having fun." Obviously he had already forgiven and forgotten my terrible transgression against him.

But I dreaded the older man's gaze, which followed my every move. I tried to say "Thank you," but his eyes were filled with sorrow and disappointment. I muttered an awkward apology and the stranger said simply, "You should not have left him alone to do this difficult thing. It would not have been asked of you."

With that, the dream ended, and I shot upright in bed. My pillow was stained, whether with perspiration or tears I do not know. I threw off the covers and ran to the little metal camp cot that was my son's bed. There on my knees and through my tears I cradled him in my arms and spoke to him while he slept. I told him that every dad makes mistakes but that they don't mean to. I told him it wasn't his fault that I had had a bad day. I told him that when boys are five or fifteen, dads sometimes forget and think they are fifty. I told him that I wanted him to be a small boy for a long, long time, because all too soon he would grow up and be a man and wouldn't be playing on the floor with his toys when I came home. I told him that I loved him and his mother and his sister more than anything in the world and that whatever challenges we had in life we would face them together. I told him that never again would I withhold my affection or my forgiveness from him, and never, I prayed, would he withhold them from me. I told him I was honored to be his father and that I would try with all my heart to be worthy of such a great responsibility.[2]

Generally speaking, Latter-day Saint parents do a marvelous job of raising righteous children. But we can do better. Unfortunately, about a third of the high school students we surveyed in the United

States, Great Britain, and Mexico reported that their mothers and fathers regularly used love withdrawal to discipline them. They reported that their parents would not even look at them, let alone speak to them, for days and even weeks.

Two particular consequences to love withdrawal and guilt induction emerged in the comments from young people. First, these two types of control erode the relationship between parents and children. The parent is saying, "I love you but only when you say and do what I want you to say and do."

Teenagers who have been repeatedly told how much they have disappointed their parents will feel unworthy of their parents' love and will withdraw from them. Inducing guilt may be punishment, but it isn't discipline. When the emotional connection between parent and child is weakened, parental influence in the life of the child is significantly diminished.

A second negative consequence of these two techniques is that they effectively degrade the development of psychological autonomy and create self-doubt. This may lead teens to feel that they are dumb, worthless, and unacceptable. They give up their individuality and become exactly what their parents want them to be to try to win back their love. Because these teens lack confidence in their own thoughts, feelings, and perceptions, depression, low academic achievement, thoughts of suicide, eating disorders, and other negative behaviors follow.

In the parable of the prodigal son, the son's demand for his inheritance showed disrespect for his upbringing, shamed the family, and may have placed economic hardship on his father. Nevertheless, when the humbled son returned, the father ran to meet him, took him in his arms, placed the family ring on his finger, and killed the fatted calf to celebrate his return.

This does not mean parents should accept evil ideas or sinful behavior, but they must continue to love the prodigals and express confidence in their return to righteousness. Acceptance as a beloved son or daughter is critical for teens to increase their psychological autonomy. Parental love and acceptance must be "stronger than the cords of death" (D&C 121:44).

We asked older parents what they had done when raising their children that they now regretted. Several confessed that they wished they had not been so controlling. They did not specify behavioral or psychological control, but they probably did both. Several of the parents can now see a lack of confidence in the children they overcontrolled. They came to understand, sometimes after painful and discouraging experiences, that nothing of real enduring value comes by psychological control, excessive guilt induction, or love withdrawal.

Encourage Children to Share Feelings, Opinions, and Ideas

One important thing that parents can do is to create a supportive environment in which they invite their children to share ideas. Time should be set aside for the family to gather and discuss what is going on in each other's lives. The mood should be relaxed and supportive so that teenagers feel comfortable and confident in sharing ideas and feelings. Dinnertime, family home evening, rides up the canyon, family service projects, and similar activities offer an opportunity for this type of environment.

Not surprisingly, researchers have found that teenagers who share an evening dinner hour with their family have significantly lower rates of delinquency and higher academic achievement. It is clear that these benefits come more from the emotional connection and the psychological autonomy fostered by family communication than from nutritional meals.

One young woman said she could talk about anything for as long as she wanted. "It was good to have deep, quality conversations with my father," she said. In contrast, another college-age young adult complained that her father stifled open communication:

> My dad's temper was scary, and he is always right. I still am unable to stick up for myself because he doesn't listen to or accept my

arguments. He sees them as talking back. I wish I could talk through problems and that I wasn't so scared of disapproval. Moreover, nothing seems to be good enough, and he thinks I am a total rebel—but I am a total Molly Mormon.

Within a relaxed setting, parents can encourage discussion that will build psychological autonomy by asking non-threatening questions such as, "How did things go at school today?" or "What did you think of last night's basketball game?" Questions with deeper meaning can follow: "What did you think of Sister Smith's testimony in fast meeting today?" "How do you feel about your algebra teacher who gave you a C?" "I heard on the news today that teen sex is prevalent among high school students. How are things in your school?"

At times your children will reply to such questions by rolling their eyes, grunting, or simply replying, "I don't know." But if you persevere, your teenagers will open up and share their feelings, hopes, fears, dreams, desires, and testimonies. Open, two-way communication is the genesis of helping teenagers develop psychological independence. Many of your conversations with them will concern trivial issues, but even trivial conversations can give you an opportunity to subtly share your cherished beliefs, values, ideas, and principles.

Living in a family exposes teenagers to many of their parents' opinions and feelings. It is part of daily living, but parents who encourage their teenage children to share their thoughts will be able to maximize their influence on the values and principles their children internalize.

Accept Your Child's Ideas and Opinions

Occasionally children may say something or express a feeling that is totally off the wall. We may wonder how our own flesh and blood could express such a stupid or outlandish idea. The real test of effective parenting at such times is to bite our tongue and fight the temptation to put teens in their place, letting them know in no uncertain terms that their idea is unacceptable.

If we react with, "That is the dumbest thing I have ever heard," we will soon discover that our children will not be willing to share ideas and feelings. We need to remember that children are children—whether they are nine or nineteen—and allow them time to grow and mature.

In response to the dumb things our own teenagers have said and done, we have declared, "Well, their brains aren't fully developed." Although said in jest, the statement is true. Neuroscience has shown that the brain—particularly the frontal lobe that controls reasoning and emotions—isn't fully developed until we reach our mid-twenties. We can't chalk up all of our teens' inappropriate sentiments and behavior to neuroscience, but it is helpful for parents to understand that just as children's bodies grow and develop, so do their minds and emotions.

A fifteen-year-old may have the physical stature of a fifty-year-old, but he doesn't reason, think, or feel like one. Sound ideas, emotional maturity, and the development of conventional morality take time and experience to fully appear. A daughter who appreciated her father's patience said:

> I had very good communications with my parents, especially my dad. I could tell him anything. He would listen to me, and if I ever told him something I did that he didn't approve of, he wouldn't yell, he would just tell me he was disappointed. I never wanted to let him down, and he was always so proud of me even though I've never been perfect.

When youth express weird, off-the-wall, unrighteous, or wicked ideas, parents need to keep their cool and not terminate the discussion with an angry outburst. It's better to respond with, "That's an interesting idea." That simple sentence has served many parents well over the years as an initial reaction to strange ideas expressed by children. This low-emotion, noncommittal response keeps the dialogue going and encourages the child to explain more fully why he feels a certain way.

If our children are reluctant to open up and share their feelings, we can ask, "Why do you think this is a good idea?" or "Why do you feel that way?"

Parents need not accept inappropriate ideas, opinions, or feelings, but they do need to accept their children's right to think. The job of a parent is to guide, teach, and lead children away from false doctrine and spiritually destructive philosophies. Parents can respect opinions and feelings and still seek to shape their children's views.

A surprising number of LDS youth in our studies articulated how their parents frustrated their attempts to expand their psychological autonomy by rejecting out of hand their ideas, opinions, and feelings. One young woman noted:

> One of my parents was very domineering and opinionated in many respects. If you disagree with them, get ready to have a debate to the death or give up to avoid trouble. I didn't feel like open opinions were welcome. There was one "right" opinion, and you better be sure yours matched it. It took coming to college to learn the true meaning of freedom of expression and thought.

A young man shared a similar experience:

> Dad was opinionated and felt he was right almost always. He is also very smart, and so when I presented a different viewpoint or argument, he would always swat it down. I don't think that he ever took me seriously. His opinions ended up being mine.

One young man explained how his father defined many of his opinions as unrighteous:

Any opinion different from my dad's was considered unrighteous. He had a gospel answer for any controversy or idea. Any character trait different than what he thought he had was unrighteous.

Another young man felt that his dad rejected his ideas out of hand simply because he was young: "I hate how my dad won't listen to anything I say—my ideas, my expressions—just because I am a 'kid.'" A BYU student still painfully recalled how his parents stifled his psychological autonomy:

My parents often discouraged ideas or plans that they deemed impractical. I wish they had supported some of my fanciful and impractical ideas. It would have shown me that they trusted my judgment and loyalty to good principles. In some ways I wish they had let me take more chances. Like when I was in the sixth grade I was frustrated with my paper route. I told my parents I wanted to quit and write a book to make money. My mom said that was a foolish idea. I wish she had entertained the idea and encouraged me to take risks like writing a book.

In characterizing parents who suppressed meaningful conversations and exchange of ideas, youth used such words as "domineering," "opinionated," "self-righteous," "closed-minded," and "authoritarian." Such parents retard the growth of their children into competent young adults capable of living successful lives.

Few teens wrote about how their parents guided their personality development. Nor did many parents describe how they fostered psychological autonomy. Most teens and parents probably take such parental behavior as normal and not worthy of comment.

One young woman recounted how her parents fostered her psychological autonomy and what it meant for her future:

> We talked about everything—politics, literature, religion, sports, cartoons, etc. We were almost encouraged to disagree and form our own opinions. My dad sort of "baited" us into arguing. Even if we disagreed at the end, it was okay. The bottom line for everything was (after discussion) what would be the best or right decision. That became my decision.

A young man noted similar encouragement from his father:

> My parents tried hard to let me know that they were my friends. By that I don't mean they were my "pals" but that they let me know often that I could come to them with my concerns, worries, happiness, etc. My dad, from the time I was small, would ask me, "What do you think?" Oftentimes I didn't have a thing on my mind, but as I grew older I did have things on my mind, and it was a natural progression for me to tell my dad what was on my mind when he asked. My mother also listened.

Teenagers who were not allowed the opportunity to express their ideas had limited confidence in their abilities. On the other hand, families that encouraged their children to explore different ideas and to test them against important moral, spiritual, and ethical family values produced youth who had confidence in their own ideas, opinions, and feelings.

Help Your Teenager Explore Ideas and Consequences

Once parents have calmly listened to their children's ideas, feelings, opinions, or perceptions, they should focus on why they feel or believe as they do. "That is an interesting idea. Why do you believe that?" is one way to continue dialogue. Questions such as "What if everyone felt that way or believed that?" will encourage youth to think about the consequences of their ideas. Within the context of such a discussion, parents should share their feelings, ideas, and opinions and *why they feel or believe as they do.* Relevant experiences from mother and father add insight to a topic.

Such discussions provide ideal settings to teach values and principles consistent with the gospel. But parents should save the trump card of bearing testimony only for serious issues. Whether a high school senior should grow a beard doesn't merit mother and father bearing testimony as to how wicked a beard is and the detrimental consequences. On the other hand, bearing testimony is certainly justified if a child is considering experimenting with premarital sex. Subtle guidance and gentle persuasion will nurture attitudes and feelings much more effectively than outbursts of criticism or solemn declarations.

Our children are looking for guidance in adopting the beliefs, values, and principles they will use to guide their daily actions. By discussing their concerns and allowing them to speak their minds, parents have a golden opportunity to guide the development of psychological autonomy. Never allowing children the right or the forum to express or explore their ideas closes lines of communication and limits meaningful parental guidance. Young people who feel their ideas and thoughts have been ridiculed or summarily dismissed by their parents usually seek out a peer group that will listen to them and respect and give credibility to their opinions and feelings.

Allow Your Children to Be People of Worth

Parents should not try to relive their lives or satisfy their unfulfilled dreams though the lives of their children. Playing on the basketball team, participating in the school band, or being a cheerleader, star debater, or class valedictorian may have been a life or death issue to parents in their youth but may hold no attraction to their children.

We are all familiar with fathers who are obsessed with making their sons into star athletes or who insist that their sons follow them into the family business. We also are familiar with mothers who are just as obsessed with making their daughters into beauty queens or cheerleaders. Children should be allowed to have their own teenage experiences and pursue their own interests.

"They allowed me to be who I wanted to be, yet encouraged me to keep my life within the bounds of the gospel," one young man explained. A young woman noted the same experience: "They let me be my own person. They didn't expect me to be the best but always gave me motivation to keep going in my commitments."

We should encourage our children to participate in a variety of wholesome activities and to test their interests and abilities. We should also share our own experiences to provide insight and motivation. But teenagers need to decide for themselves which activities to pursue and how hard to pursue them. By allowing our children the right to live their own lives and follow their own interests, we help them become confident in their abilities to accomplish their dreams and goals in life.

Psychological autonomy is probably unfamiliar to most parents. But they intuitively understand the importance of their children internalizing important guiding values and principles. Parents can significantly cultivate psychological autonomy by encouraging children of all ages to share their thoughts and ideas.

Mom and Dad should avoid overreacting to inappropriate ideas and help young people explore the source of their thoughts and determine the consequences those thoughts may have. Such experiences will assist our children to mature into competent young adults who are committed to and active in the Church, who maximize their educational and career opportunities, and who are likely to find greater happiness and fulfillment in their marriages and families. Certainly that is what we would want for them.

Notes

1. *Messages of the First Presidency,* comp. James R. Clark, 6 vols. (Salt Lake City: Bookcraft, 1965–75), 3:54.

2. Jeffrey R. Holland, "Within the Clasp of Your Arms," *Ensign,* May 1983, 36–38.

Chapter 10

Don't Give Up

Several years ago the dramatic rescue of a hiker stranded in the middle of a raging river was televised on a network newscast. The hiker had been traveling down a canyon when a sudden thunderstorm and a resulting flash flood caught him by surprise and left him clinging to a small, but tall, rock outcropping. What was once a big rock in the canyon suddenly became a veritable island surrounded by rising, swirling water. With sheer cliffs on both sides, it was the only "high ground" available.

As the minutes passed, the hiker's high ground grew smaller and smaller. Fortunately, he was able to call for emergency help with his mobile telephone, and a search and rescue team scrambled into action.

It was soon apparent that the only way to save the stranded hiker was to fly a helicopter into the canyon, drop a line to him, secure him with a safety harness, and hoist him to the helicopter. This would have been an extraordinarily risky endeavor under the best of conditions, but amidst the rain and gusts of wind it was a gamble at best.

While flying up the canyon, the helicopter pilot quickly realized that it would be impossible to hover over the hiker. His only hope of rescuing the hiker was to fly as slowly and as close to him as safely possible and have him grab on to one of the landing bars. The hiker literally would have to hang on for dear life while the pilot flew to an area where he could drop the hiker to safety.

It was an amazing sight to see the stranded hiker grab on to the landing bar as the helicopter slowly flew overhead and then dangle precariously as the helicopter picked up speed and altitude. The hiker had no safety belt, no helmet, and nothing to secure himself to the helicopter or to protect himself if he fell. His survival depended on his ability to just hang on.

The story had a happy ending, with the hiker safely reunited with his family and friends and the brave helicopter pilot hailed as a hero.

"How were you able to do it?" a reporter later asked the rescued hiker. "I really didn't have any choice," he responded. "I had to hang on or die."

The formula for safety was as simple as that—hang on for dear life! Don't let go until you reach safety. Parenting is like that. You do what you have to do to survive, and sometimes that means just hanging on for dear life.

Raising a family is not always as dramatic or full of white-knuckle excitement as a helicopter rescue. It's more like a roller-coaster ride. Sometimes it's fun and leisurely. Other times it's full of heart-stopping thrills and moments of gut-wrenching panic. But no matter what the roller-coaster ride of parenting is like, you can't jump off.

"Do the very best you can," President Gordon B. Hinckley counseled all parents, especially those who have experienced the heartache of children who go astray. "And when you have done that, you just place the matter in the hands of the Lord. Go forward with faith. Nobody is lost until somebody has given up. You stay with it."[1]

"After All We Can Do"

The Book of Mormon prophet Nephi taught, "It is by grace that we are saved, *after all we can do*" (2 Nephi 25:23; emphasis added). That is true not only when it comes to salvation through the atonement of Jesus Christ but also as a parenting principle. "After all we can do" as parents, how our children turn out, both here and hereafter, will ultimately be up to them and the Lord. "All we can do" is do the best parenting we can and then, as President Hinckley admonished, "place the matter in the hands of the Lord." That, however, is easier said than done.

"All we can do" and "do[ing] the very best [we] can" are intimidating, even overwhelming, statements. Even the best parents have regrets. All of us, at some time or another, wish we had done things differently with our children—expressed our love more, raised our voices less, been more involved in their lives, disciplined them more consistently. The list could go on and on.

Satan seeks to discourage all parents but especially those whose hearts have been broken by a child's poor choices, sinful behavior, or unresponsiveness to gospel teachings. Statements such as "I wish I would have," or "Things would be better if," or "We shouldn't have" can become emotional billy clubs with which we beat ourselves over the head. Regret doesn't yield anything positive by itself. Only when we learn from our mistakes, try to do better, develop new skills, and continue to do what we know is right, instead of giving up and giving in to discouragement, does parental self-inspection benefit our families.

One father, whose children were already raised and happily married, expressed some parental regret to his wife. "I wish now that I had hugged my daughters more when they were young and had expressed my love to them more often." Knowing that expressions of regret aren't as valuable as behavioral changes, his wife replied, "You know, it's never too late. I'm sure they would appreciate it even now."

The father's efforts to do a little better and to try a little harder yielded great rewards for his family. Efforts to improve as parents are part of our ongoing responsibility to do "all we can do." We need to do the best we know and when we know better, we need to do better.

Sometimes "all we can do" for our children—especially the prodigals who won't listen or be influenced by our love or standards—is to continually pray for them. Whether they are fourteen or forty, faithful or faithless, we can pray for them. In our family prayers and our personal petitions, we can pour out our heart for them, asking the Eternal Father who knows and loves them even more than we do to care for them, protect them, and touch their hearts.

Even when our children won't listen to us, our Father in Heaven will. As the apostle James declared, "The effectual fervent prayer of a righteous man [or woman, father, or mother] availeth much" (James 5:16). Praying for our children is certainly easier than being patient with our children. Yet patience is one of the most important parental "all we can do" things. Whatever their age or stage, we need to pray for them as we seek to cultivate the patience of Job.

President Hinckley has observed that our children "may do, in the years that come, some things you would not want them to do, but be patient, be patient."[2] Patience is linked with faith. When we become impatient that our children haven't yet turned around and done what they were taught at home, we exhibit a lack of faith in God's awareness of our family challenges, in his personal acquaintance with each of his children, and in his ability to do what needs to be done.

Because we can't see the end from the beginning, we are impatient with our children when their spiritual progress is slower than we would like. In our impatience we sometimes say or do things to speed up the process, which may be counterproductive. Elder Neal A. Maxwell described such impatience as "too much anxious opening of the oven door," which causes the cake to fall instead of rise, and "pulling up the daisies to see how the roots are doing."[3] As hard as it is, we must be willing to accept the Lord's will, as well as his timetable. We need to recognize that he is not yet done with our children who have strayed from the path.

Hanging on to our children in our divine yet demanding role as parents requires even more than prayer, patience, and perseverance. Striving to be righteous in our own lives—exercising faith in the

Savior, keeping our covenants, repenting of our sins, rendering service to the Church and our fellowman— is also part of the "all we can do" as parents. Such efforts reflect both our love for the Lord and commitment to his gospel and our love for our children and generations yet to come.

Righteousness is not just for self; it is also for the everlasting family—our everlasting family. Each act of parental faithfulness affects, influences, and blesses the entire family. Elder Jeffrey R. Holland taught this important parenting principle in a talk addressed to mothers in the Church. His words have equal application to fathers:

> If you and your husband will strive to love God and live the gospel yourselves; if you will plead for that guidance and comfort of the Holy Spirit promised to the faithful; if you will go to the temple to both make and claim the promises of the most sacred covenants a woman or man can make in this world; if you will show others, including your children, the same caring, compassionate, forgiving heart you want heaven to show you; if you try your best to be the best parent you can be, you will have done all that a human being can do and all that God expects you to do.
>
> Sometimes the decision of a child or grandchild will break your heart. Sometimes expectations won't immediately be met. Every mother and father worries about that. Even that beloved and wonderfully successful parent President

Joseph F. Smith pled, "Oh! God, let me not lose my own." That is every parent's cry, and in it is something of every parent's fear. But no one has failed who keeps trying and keeps praying. You have every right to receive encouragement and to know in the end your children will call your name blessed, just like those generations of foremothers [and forefathers] before you who hoped your same hopes and felt your same fears.[4]

"They That Be with Us Are More Than They That Be with Them"

An inspiring story in the Old Testament, though rarely viewed in this context, can serve as a significant source of comfort, guidance, and strength for parents. It is the account of divine protection afforded the prophet Elisha when he was surrounded by the Syrian armies.

The kingdom of Israel had been invaded from the north by the Syrians. Under the inspiration of the Lord, Elisha had warned the Israelite king of the invasion and counseled him on how to wage war against the Syrians. When the king of Syria was apprised of the fact that Elisha was counseling the king of Israel regarding the positions and strategies of the Syrian army, he sent horses, chariots, and soldiers to surround the city and capture him.

"And when the servant of the man of God was risen early, and gone forth, behold, an host compassed the city both with horses and chariots. And his servant said unto him, Alas, my master! How shall we do?"

In our modern vernacular, the young servant was asking, "How are we going to get out of this mess? We are totally surrounded!"

Elisha's response may have caused the young man to think that the prophet was delusional, in denial, or talking in his sleep. "Fear not," Elisha declared, "for they that be with us are more than they that be with them" (2 Kings 6:16). How could that be? As far as the young servant could see, he beheld a great host of Syrian soldiers armed with swords and spears and riding warhorses and chariots. How could anybody in his right mind declare, "They that be with us are more than they that be with them"?

The situation must have appeared hopeless to the young man as he surveyed the odds—one young man and one aged man against an entire army! Perhaps they should give up—surrender to their formidable foe.

Elisha must have seen the fear and confusion in his servant's eyes. "And Elisha prayed, and said, Lord, I pray thee, open his eyes, that he may see. And the Lord opened the eyes of the young man; and he saw: and, behold, the mountain was full of horses and chariots of fire round about Elisha" (2 Kings 6:17).

If our spiritual eyes could be opened as were the

eyes of the servant of Elisha, we too would discover that we are not left alone or forsaken in our battles against the evils of the world. There is more power found in the gospel of Jesus Christ than among Satan and all his minions. We may feel surrounded and badly outnumbered by the enemies of righteousness as we seek to raise our children, but the Lord has blessed us with great resources to strengthen and protect our families.

We are blessed to have the support and strength of an entire team composed of prophets, apostles, leaders, teachers, advisers, friends, and extended family members. Each contributes to our efforts to raise our children up unto the Lord. Their support encourages and strengthens us, especially when we feel helpless or hopeless. The power of our team far surpasses that of our opponent. Besides, we already know the outcome. God will be victorious. We need to keep that in mind when it seems we are losing the battle.

In addition to the divine assistance afforded parents in the form of inspired counsel from prophets and apostles, the programs and activities of the Church, and the guidance of the Holy Ghost, parents also receive help from beyond the veil.

"It may very well be that there are more helpful sources [for parents] at work than we know," President James E. Faust said. "I believe there is a strong familial pull as the influence of beloved ancestors continues with us from the other side of the veil."[5]

The Lord has promised faithful parents and individuals, "I will go before your face. I will be on your right hand and on your left, and my Spirit shall be in your hearts, and mine angels round about you, to bear you up" (D&C 84:88).

The Lord does not forsake families in these troubled times. Parents are not left alone in their weighty and eternally significant responsibilities. Probably more than we realize, we are receiving help from beyond the veil in guiding, directing, and protecting our families. Undoubtedly, there is at least as much, if not more, love and concern for family members in the hearts of departed loved ones on the other side of the veil as there is in the hearts of earthly parents.

This important doctrine can be illustrated by a touching story from the life of Elder Bruce R. McConkie. When his beloved father, Oscar W. McConkie Sr., was about to die, he gathered his family to express his love and to testify anew of the truths of the gospel. "I am going to die," he declared. "When I die I shall not cease to love you. I shall not cease to pray for you. I shall not cease to labor in your behalf."[6]

What a wonderful promise of help and hope for families! This doctrine gives us strength to carry on, even amidst discouragement and disappointment. It powerfully reminds us that we must never give up, for there are unseen others laboring and loving with us, and they never give up!

The Redemptive Power of the Covenant

Even with the promise of divine assistance from beyond the veil, some parents may still feel that there is no hope for reclaiming a lost son or daughter. It may appear that all parental efforts have failed, that all familial support has eroded, that no divine ear is listening to their pleadings, that hope for an Alma-like miracle (Mosiah 27:10–14) has faded. But there is a power afforded to families greater than all earthly efforts of home and Church combined. It is the redemptive power of the covenant. Of this power, Elder Boyd K. Packer testified:

> It is a great challenge to raise a family in the darkening mists of our moral environment.
>
> We emphasize that the greatest work you will do will be within the walls of your home (see Harold B. Lee, *Ensign,* July 1973, 98), and that "no other success can compensate for failure in the home" (David O. McKay, *Improvement Era,* June 1964, 445).
>
> The measure of our success as parents, however, will not rest solely on how our children turn out. That judgment would be just only if we could raise our families in a perfectly moral environment, and that now is not possible.

It is not uncommon for responsible parents to lose one of their children, for a time, to influences over which they have no control. They agonize over rebellious sons or daughters. They are puzzled why they are so helpless when they have tried so hard to do what they should.

It is my conviction that those wicked influences one day will be overruled. . . . We cannot overemphasize the value of temple marriage, the binding ties of the sealing ordinance, and the standards of worthiness required of them. When parents keep the covenants they have made at the altar of the temple, their children will forever be bound to them.[7]

We do not fully understand how all of this operates and will eventually unfold, but we are assured of the reality of this hope-anchoring promise. Several prophets and apostles in this dispensation have taught this doctrine.[8] President Lorenzo Snow promised parents:

You that are mourning about your children straying away will have your sons and your daughters. If you succeed in passing through these trials and afflictions and receive a resurrection, you will, by the power of the Priesthood, work and labor, as the Son of God has, until you get all your sons and daughters in the path of exaltation and glory. This is just as sure as that the sun rose this morning over yonder mountains. Therefore, mourn not because all your sons and daughters do not follow in the path that you have marked out to them, or give heed to your counsels. Inasmuch as we succeed in securing eternal glory, and stand as saviors, and as kings and priests to our God, we will save our posterity. . . .

God will have His own way in His own time, and He will accomplish His purposes in the salvation of His sons and daughters. . . . God bless you, brethren and sisters. *Do not be discouraged* is the word I wish to pass to you; but remember that righteousness and joy in the Holy Ghost is what you and I have the privilege of possessing at all times.[9]

What a glorious promise! What comforting and strengthening counsel to parents! If we are true and faithful to our covenants and do "all we can do" in loving and leading our families in righteousness, we have claim on the redemptive power of our covenants not only for ourselves but also for our children. When we really understand this doctrine and believe these promises, we can face with faith and courage the challenge of rearing righteous children in an increasingly wicked world.

Because we know that "the family is central to the Creator's plan for the eternal destiny of His children,"[10] we can, with absolute spiritual assurance, declare, as did Winston Churchill when he rallied his countrymen on June 4, 1940, against relentless Nazi attacks, "We shall never surrender." The stakes are even higher today as we face a worse enemy than the Nazis and a battle more critical than the Battle of

Britain. We are experiencing an all-out attack on the everlasting family—our eternal family. We must never give up. However long and hard the road, we must never surrender. We must never lose hope because the outcome is certain.

We have an absolute conviction that the gospel of Jesus Christ is God's greatest gift to the families of the world. It is the greatest help for parents and children. It is guaranteed. It really works! Our prayer for your family and our families is best expressed in the heartfelt prayer for all parents offered by our beloved prophet, President Gordon B. Hinckley. May we all come to know and feel the fulfillment of these words as we seek to fulfill our divine callings as mothers and fathers.

> O God, the Eternal Father, bless the parents to teach with love and patience and encouragement those who are most precious, the children who have come from Thee, that together they might be safeguarded and directed for good and, in the process of growth, bring blessings to the world of which they will be a part, I pray in the name of Jesus Christ, amen.[11]

Notes

1. "At Home with the Hinckleys," *Ensign*, October 2003, 25.

2. Gordon B. Hinckley, *Teachings of Gordon B. Hinckley* (Salt Lake City: Deseret Book, 1997), 422.

3. Neal A. Maxwell, "Patience," *1979 Devotional Speeches of the Year* (Provo, Utah: Brigham Young University Press, 1980), 216, 218.

4. Jeffrey R. Holland, "Because She Is a Mother," *Ensign,* May 1997, 36.

5. James E. Faust, "Dear Are the Sheep That Have Wandered," *Ensign,* May 2003, 62.

6. In Robert L. Millet, *When a Child Wanders* (Salt Lake City: Deseret Book, 1996), 133.

7. Boyd K. Packer, "Our Moral Environment," *Ensign,* May 1992, 68.

8. See Brigham Young, in *Journal of Discourses,* 26 vols. (London: Latter-day Saints' Book Depot, 1854–86), 11:215; Orson F. Whitney, Conference Report, April 1929, 110; James E. Faust, "Dear Are the Sheep that Have Wandered," *Ensign,* May 2003, 61–68.

9. Lorenzo Snow, in *Collected Discourses,* comp. Brian H. Stuy, 5 vols. (Burbank, Calif.: BHS Publishing, 1987–92): 3:364–65.

10. The First Presidency and Council of the Twelve Apostles, "The Family—A Proclamation to the World," *Ensign,* November 1995, 102.

11. Gordon B. Hinckley, "Bring Up a Child in the Way He Should Go," *Ensign,* November 1993, 60.

About the Authors

Brent L. Top

Brent L. Top, a professor of Church history and doctrine at Brigham Young University, has been a religious educator in the Church Educational System for more than twenty-five years. He is a former associate dean of religious education and currently holds the Endowed Professorship in Moral Education at BYU. He holds a Ph.D. from BYU and is the author of several Church books and numerous articles on doctrinal, historical, sociological, and family subjects. He and his wife, Wendy, live in Pleasant Grove, Utah. They are the parents of four children and the grandparents of seven.

Bruce A. Chadwick

Bruce A. Chadwick, a professor of sociology at Brigham Young University, has been studying and writing about families for more than four decades. He is a past recipient of the prestigious Karl G. Maeser Distinguished Research Award at BYU and currently holds the Maeser Professorship in General Education. He is a former director of the Family Studies Program and the Center for the Studies of the Family at BYU. He received his Ph.D. from Washington University in St. Louis, Missouri, and has published numerous books and articles on family and sociological issues. He and his wife, Carolyn, live in Pleasant Grove, Utah. They are the parents of three children and the grandparents of seven.

Index